# *Summer in the Garden*

gardening workbooks

# *Summer in the Garden*

**Steven Bradley**

*photography by* **Anne Hyde**

RYLAND
PETERS
& SMALL

First published in Great Britain in 1998
by Ryland Peters & Small
Cavendish House
51–55 Mortimer Street
London W1N 7TD

Text © 1998 Steven Bradley

Design and illustration © 1998
Ryland Peters & Small

Printed in China
Produced by Sun Fung Offset Binding Co. Ltd

Designers **Prue Bucknall, Ashley Western**
Editors **Toria Leitch, Lesley Riley**
Production **Kate Mackillop**
Illustrators **Polly Raynes, Amanda Patton, Ann Winterbotham, David Ashby**

ISBN 1 900518 47 3

A catalogue record for this book is available
from the British Library

# contents

**introduction** 6

**new introductions** 8
lifting and planting bulbs 10
planting annuals and biennials 12
perennials 14
planting vegetables 16
routine care of vegetables 18
harvesting vegetables and herbs 19
using trees and shrubs
   in containers 20
a shrub border for
   year-round interest 22
project: summer bedding 24

**propagation** 28
cuttings 30
collecting seeds and bulbs 32
division 34
bulb scaling 36
layering 38

**seasonal pruning** 40
the essentials 42
annuals 44
shrubs 46
climbers and wall shrubs 48
roses 50
trees 52
fruit 54
hedges 56

project: training fruit trees 58
project: topiary 62

**lawn care** 66
mowing 68
weeding 70
watering 71
feeding 72
pest and disease control 73
project: planting ground
   cover 74

**routine care** 78
feeding 80
watering 82
protection 84
pests and diseases 86
controlling weeds 88
project: making a sink garden 90

**pond care** 94
pond maintenance 96
summer plantings 98
propagation 100
project: pebble pond 102

glossary 106
useful addresses 108
credits 109
index 110
acknowledgements 112

summer is usually the most colourful time of the year in the garden. Many plants begin to ensure the survival of their species by producing seeds, and in order to do this, they must flower. This first stage in producing the next generation gives the gardener the opportunity to create an ever-changing symphony of colour.

Growth is still rapid in summer, and to sustain it, much of the seasonal work during these months is aimed at keeping the plants watered and fed. At times, it may feel as if the gardener has to run in order to stand still. The lawn appears to grow overnight and is in need of constant mowing, simply to keep it looking trim. Hedges need clipping at every turn. Blooms need dead-heading, flowering shrubs need pruning, young fruit trees must be trained. No sooner has one batch of vegetable seeds been sown than another demands to be thinned or staked or moved to another site. The burgeoning growth and development of the plants seems to be matched only by the frenetic activity of the insects, weeds, and diseases that are competing with them and feeding off them.

Regardless of all the hard labour, the summer is a time when the garden can be enjoyed at close quarters. The warm weather and long evenings entice us out of doors for long periods, for work and relaxation. To the uninitiated, it may appear that nothing is actively being done at all, but the gardener knows otherwise. The time spent sitting in the garden is often used to note successful plants and planting schemes, and to record any failures or disappointments for moving or disposal. This will ensure that the same mistakes are not made next year, when the glorious technicolour experiment can be tried all over again.

Steven Bradley

# new introductions

*For most gardeners summer is an exciting time, as plants introduced in earlier seasons grow and begin to bloom. There is a sense of great anticipation, too, as ideas for new planting schemes take shape, perhaps inspired by the vast range of* plants on show at garden centres and in other people's gardens. The challenge may be to produce a display that changes with the seasons, providing colour and interest all year round. You may wish to design a new garden

*feature, such as a perennial border, or simply to increase the range of plants to be grown in containers on the deck or patio. The vegetable and herb garden creates its own excitement as new crops are sown and the first delicious produce of the season can be harvested and enjoyed.*

# Lifting and Planting Bulbs

Although gardeners often think of spring when bulbs are mentioned, there is a fair amount of work to be done in the summer, not only to take care of the now dormant spring-flowering bulbs, but also to prepare for the autumn-flowering display.

## Lifting bulbs

**1** Carefully lift 'old' spring bulbs and leave in a cool, dry place for two or three days before brushing off any soil. Trim away old roots and loose papery scales, and remove the dried stems level with the bulb 'neck'.

**2** Gently pull away any 'bulblets' from around the mother bulb; these can be used to grow new plants. Discard soft or unusually light bulbs, as they may be infested with eelworms or bulb fly maggots, or be decaying due to damage caused by fungal rots.

**3** Using clean, shallow trays or boxes lined with paper, arrange the bulbs in a single layer and put them in a cool, dry place until it is time for replanting in the autumn. Inspect the bulbs every two or three weeks and discard immediately any that show signs of fungal rot or softness, otherwise the surrounding bulbs may become infected.

## Planting autumn-flowering bulbs

Autumn-flowering bulbs are best planted in the early to middle part of the summer, when they are coming towards the end of their dormant period. They will establish themselves readily at this time, quickly putting down roots and, before long, bursting into growth.

### Autumn-flowering bulbs

| | | |
|---|---|---|
| *Amaryllis belladonna* | *Crocus sativus* | *Leucojum autumnale* |
| *Colchicum agrippinum* | *Crocus speciosus* | *Nerine bowdenii* |
| *Colchicum autumnale* | *Cyclamen hederifolium* | *Schizostylis coccinea* |
| *Crinum × powellii* | *Dierama pulcherrimum* | *Sternbergia lutea* |
| *Crocosmia masoniorum* | *Eucomis bicolor* | *Tigridia pavonia* |

Colchicum *'The Giant'*

Amaryllis belladonna

Cyclamen hederifolium

# Planting depth

The depth at which bulbs should be planted varies from as shallow as 1 cm (½in), to as deep as 25 cm (10 in), depending upon the plant. Usually, the taller the plant will grow, the deeper the bulb needs to be buried, to be sure it is securely anchored in the ground. As a rough guide, the bulb should be covered with two to three times its own depth of soil; plant a little deeper in light soil, and not quite so deep if your soil is very heavy.

# Planting

**1** Push the bulb planter or trowel into the ground with a twisting motion to cut through the soil, rather than forcing it straight in.

**2** After making the planting hole, break up the soil in the bottom with a trowel.

**3** Set the bulb in the hole in an upright position, then fill in around the bulb with soil until the surface is level. Firm in gently.

# Supporting bulbous plants

Taller bulbs, such as lilies, may need some support through the growing season to prevent the stems becoming damaged. They are usually most at risk when the flowers are starting to open, particularly if the weather becomes showery. The amount of water held in the flower can cause the plant to bend over and lie across the ground; if this happens the plant will be unable to right itself and the flowers will be spoiled. Gladioli and similar tall plants can be supported by 'earthing up'. This involves creating a mound around the base of the stem to encourage more roots to form close to the surface. Alternatively, use a cane and ties to support the plant, being sure to insert the cane on the opposite side to the developing flowers.

*A mound of soil around the base of the plant will help to stop it falling over.*

*If using a cane support, tie the stem to it with soft string or raffia.*

Gladiolus tristis *'Bowlby'*

Lilium *'Enchantment'*

Lilium candidum

# Planting Annuals and Biennials These plants

provide an enormous variety of flower colour, form and foliage texture, making them ideal candidates for planting in containers and hanging baskets; in the garden soil, they can be used to great effect massed in a bed by themselves, or as 'fillers' in gaps between shrubs and other permanent plants. By choosing suitable species and cultivars, it is possible to have flowers for a large part of the year. Often, half-hardy annuals are used for summer colour, as they are very fast growing and provide an amazing display, which may last through until the first frosts of autumn or early winter.

## Half-hardy plants for a summer display

Many summer bedding plants are half-hardy annuals whose seeds, if left to themselves, would not germinate until the early summer. Sowing seed in trays of compost in spring and keeping them under glass or on a warm windowsill means the plants will start growing early. Once the seedlings are large enough to handle without risk of damage, they can be transplanted from their seed trays into small pots. This will give them the space and food they need to keep them growing quickly. Gradually harden them off (get them used to being outside), before planting them out into their flowering site.

### Transplanting (pricking out) seedlings

**1** Select several small pots and fill to the top with a suitable compost. Using your fingers or a dibber, gently firm down the surface of the compost to 1 cm (½in) below the rim.

**2** Using a label or similar utensil, gently tease the seedlings out of the seed compost. Do this when the compost is slightly moist.

**3** Make a hole with a dibber in the centre of each pot. Then, lifting the seedlings individually, place each one root first into a hole.

**4** Water gently to settle the compost around the roots. Label the pots with the plant name and date, then place in a shaded spot.

**5** For plants destined to go into troughs and tubs, grow in 8 cm (3 in) plastic pots and plunge them into the decorative container. The plant's roots will grow through the bottom of the pot into the compost.

**6** After flowering, the plant can easily be removed by twisting the pot from side to side to sever any roots that have pushed through the drainage holes. You can then drop a replacement plant neatly into the hole.

# Sowing hardy plants for a spring display

As well as annuals, many hardy biennials are used for outdoor display in the spring, as are perennials that are grown and treated as biennials. All are raised in the summer and grown through the autumn and winter before flowering. Due to the long period before flowering, these plants are usually sown in a seedbed during the early summer, then the seedlings are transplanted into a nursery bed about six or eight weeks later. Here they will grow on, producing stems and leaves, until they are large enough to be planted into the display beds in mid-autumn.

## Sowing seed outdoors

The seeds are sown in straight lines or 'drills' so that the seedlings are in rows about 20 cm (8 in) apart. A groove is cut in the soil (the depth depends on the seed involved) and the seed scattered along the bottom of the drill. Seeds should be sown as thinly as possible to reduce the need for thinning seedlings later. Sowing in drills is most commonly used for plants grown in nursery beds and transplanted later into permanent positions.

## Lifting the seedlings

As soon as the seedlings have grown to a manageable size, about 8 cm (3 in) high, or when they have developed three to five true leaves, they are ready for transplanting into the nursery bed. Water the rows of seedlings a day before they are lifted to help the plants to establish quickly when moved. Lift the seedling plants with a small garden fork, to reduce the risk of injury to the roots, and hold them by their leaves to avoid damaging the soft stems or the delicate root hairs.

## Transplanting

Space out the seedlings 20 cm (8 in) apart, in rows 30 cm (12 in) apart. The lowest leaf should sit just above soil level. Firm the plants gently and water them immediately to settle the soil around the roots. Giving the seedlings plenty of space will encourage them to produce shoots close to the base, forming stocky multi-stemmed plants.

### Hardy biennials

Columbine *(Aquilegia)*
Daisy *(Bellis perennis)*
Forget-me-not *(Myosotis)*
Foxglove *(Digitalis)*
Honesty *(Lunaria)*
Lupin *(Lupinus)*
Pansy *(Viola)*
Ruby chard *(Beta vulgaris)*
Sweet William *(Dianthus)*
Wallflower *(Erysimum cheiri)*

Aquilegia vulgaris

*Lupin*

# Perennials
A large number of perennials produce the majority of their flowers through the summer months, and can be used to provide a riot of colour and plenty of interest, filling in any bare patches. These plants can be purchased growing in containers in the summer and planted immediately, but be sure to keep them well watered until they are growing strongly.

## Creating an instant display

The main advantage of buying perennials in the summer is that the plants can be seen in flower and close to their ultimate height and spread. This will be invaluable if you need to fill a gap in a group of plants, or want to hide another, early-flowering perennial that is no longer looking its best. It will be useful, too, if you are planning a border from scratch, as you should be able to get a clear impression of how the plants will look all together. There is no need to stick rigidly to the rule of putting the shortest plants at the front of the border, and the tallest ones at the back – a change in height often lends extra interest.

## Colour scheming

There are numerous ways of using colour to create a theme within the display. You can, for instance, give a border a rainbow theme, starting at one end with plants in shades of violet, merging into blues, and changing through greens and yellows on to oranges and reds. This may be effective for a long border, giving it a feeling of harmony and drawing the eye easily from end to end. Another option could be colour groupings within a number of separate borders around the garden: blue, pink and white; pale yellow, cream and salmon shades; purple, magenta and brown-purple shades; or maroon, red, orange and deep yellows. Or you could adopt a temperature theme: borders in 'hot' colours, which include reds, yellows and oranges, can look spectacular in a warm, sunny position; for a 'cool' border in a semi-shaded site, use blues, greens and whites.

---

### Plants for a cool border in semi-shade

| | |
|---|---|
| *Agapanthus* Headbourne hybrids | *Geum* 'Rubin' |
| *Alchemilla mollis* | *Iris sibirica* |
| *Anaphalis yedoensis* | *Liriope muscari* |
| *Astrantia major* | *Nepeta* 'Six Hills Giant' |
| *Centranthus ruber* var. *coccineus* | *Polemonium* 'Sapphire' |
| *Dicentra spectabilis* 'Alba' | *Pulmonaria angustifolia* subsp. *azurea* |
| *Euphorbia amygdaloides* var. *robbiae* | *Scabiosa caucasica* 'Butterfly Blue' |
| *Geranium* 'Johnson's Blue' | *Tradescantia* 'Osprey' |
| | *Yucca flaccida* 'Ivory' |

Geranium *'Johnson's Blue'*

---

### Plants for a hot border in a warm, sunny position

| | |
|---|---|
| *Achillea filipendulina* 'Gold Plate' | *Ligularia* 'The Rocket' |
| *Bergenia* 'Morgenrote' | *Oenothera missouriensis* |
| *Cosmos atrosanguineus* | *Penstemon* 'Garnet' |
| *Crocosmia masoniorum* | *Potentilla* 'Gibson's Scarlet' |
| *Dahlia* 'Bishop of Llandaff' | *Rudbeckia fulgida* var. *sullivanii* 'Goldsturm' |
| *Dianthus* 'Christopher' | *Saponaria ocymoides* |
| *Hemerocallis* 'Stella de Oro' | *Schizostylis coccinea* 'Major' |
| *Incarvillea delavayi* | *Sedum* 'Autumn Joy' |
| *Kniphofia caulescens* | *Trollius* 'Orange Princess' |

Rudbeckia fulgida

# Planting a perennial border

When choosing plants, make sure that the colours blend well, and that the ultimate size of the plants is in scale with the border and the surrounding garden. It is essential that the plants are of good quality, producing strong healthy growth from the base or through the compost. Reject any plants that have obvious signs of pests or disease, a large population of weeds growing in the compost, or broken or damaged stems or branches.

## How deep to plant

Correct planting depth is very important: plants with a fibrous root system, such as asters, should have the topmost root about 1 cm (½in) below soil level; those with a thick fleshy root, such as acanthus, or those with a cluster or crown of buds, such as hostas, should have the top of the root at around 2.5 cm (1 in) below soil level.

## Planting container-grown perennials

**1** Before planting begins, water the container thoroughly to make sure the plant's roots are moist, especially if the weather conditions are hot and dry.

**2** Dig a planting hole large enough to accommodate the plant's root system.

**3** Holding the plant by its stem or leaves, gently pull it from the container.

**4** Gently remove the top 1 cm (½in) of compost from the root ball and discard it (this layer will contain most weed seeds and moss). Take care not to break up the root ball, as this would disturb the plant, but you can cut back any long, coiled roots.

**5** Holding the plant by the root ball, place it in the hole so that it sits securely at the bottom. Do make sure the hole is big enough: the plant will quickly become established if its roots can push easily through the soil.

**6** Pull the soil back into the hole with a trowel, and firm gently around the plant with your hands. Make sure that the surface of the compost is covered by soil, and leave a slight depression around the base of the stem. Check that the plant is securely in place.

**7** Water immediately after planting, filling the depression around the base. Keep the plant well watered until it is established.

# Planting Vegetables

For most gardeners, the purpose of growing vegetables is to provide a constant supply of fresh edible produce, and to achieve this the summer must be a period for planning as well as growing. Many of the vegetables planted in the spring will soon be ready for harvest, while many that mature through the autumn, winter and spring of the following year will need to be propagated and the young plants raised in the summer. Other rapidly growing crops will need to be sown at regular, frequent intervals to make sure the continuity of supply is not broken.

## Successional sowing

Quick-growing crops, especially the short-term salad vegetables such as lettuces and radishes, are the ones where gluts and shortages are the most likely to occur, but to a large extent this situation can be avoided by careful planning and sowing batches of seed on a regular basis.

| Vegetables for successional sowing | |
| --- | --- |
| Beans | Lettuces |
| French | Radishes |
| runner | Spinach |
| Chinese cabbage | Spring onions |

### Timing
This can be difficult to gauge, especially for the inexperienced gardener, as many plants will mature more rapidly in warmer weather. You can work out when to sow from the date you hope to harvest the crop, by counting back the number of weeks needed for the plants to grow; most of this information can be found on the seed packet. Sow the next batch of seed when the previous batch has germinated and emerged through the soil.

## Sowing vegetable seeds

**1** Firm and roughly level an area of seedbed using a large-toothed rake. Add a base dressing of fertilizer and rake it into the soil.

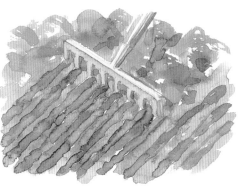

**2** Insert a line and use a draw hoe to make a seed drill up to 2 cm (¾in) deep. It needs to be the same depth all along its length.

**3** Space the seeds evenly all along the bottom of the drill, then rake loose soil over the top. Check that the seeds are covered with a layer of earth, then gently press down the soil until it is firm. Write the name of the plant on a label and push it into the earth at one end of the row.

# Transplanting seedlings from beds or trays

After germination, seedlings are often too close together and they will need to be moved (transplanted) to a different site where they will have plenty of space to grow and mature. The seedlings are usually ready for transplanting when they are about 8 cm (3 in) high, each with four or five leaves.

| Seedlings for transplanting | |
|---|---|
| Broccoli | Calabrese |
| Sprouting | Cauliflower |
| Chinese | Autumn |
| Brussels sprouts | Winter |
| Cabbage | Spring |
| Chinese | Kale |
| Winter | Leeks |
| Spring | Lettuce |

**1** Dig a planting hole that is large enough to accommodate the root system of the seedling and, gently grasping the plant by its stem or leaves, place it in the hole, making sure that the roots are spread out evenly.

**2** Using the trowel pull the soil back into the hole around the seedling, leaving an indentation around the stem, and firm gently into place with your hands. Test the plant is secure by tugging a leaf upwards. Water immediately after planting, by filling the indentation around the base of the plant.

# Transplanting pot-grown seedlings

**1** More tender vegetables, sown in pots, need to be transplanted into a warm soil and grown through a sheet of black plastic, which will retain heat and moisture. Lay the plastic sheet over the soil and bury the edges.

**4** Pull the soil back into the hole around the plant, and firm gently into place, leaving a slight depression at the base of the stem.

**2** Cut a cross in the plastic where the plant is intended to be inserted, fold back the flaps of plastic and dig a planting hole large enough to accommodate the plant's root system. Work carefully to avoid tearing the plastic.

**5** Immediately after planting, fold the flaps of plastic back over the soil so they meet at the plant stem. Water around the base of the plant.

**3** Turn the plant upside down and remove the pot. Holding the plant by the root ball, place it in the hole.

| Pot-grown seedlings |
|---|
| Aubergine |
| Cucumber |
| Marrow |
| Peppers |
| Sweet corn |
| Tomato |

# Routine Care of Vegetables

The summer is a particularly busy time for the vegetable gardener as many of the established plants will need constant attention to produce good crops. Routine, but very important, tasks include training, staking, protecting and weeding.

## Supporting vegetables

Tall and climbing vegetables will need to be given some form of support as they grow, to prevent the stems becoming damaged or broken and to help them bear the weight of the crop.

Runner beans, broad beans and peas need to be supported on wooden sticks or bamboo canes, arranged to form a tent-like structure. These are best put into position in the spring so that the plant has something to grow up as soon as it emerges from the soil. If the supports are not yet in place, insert them as the twining stems start to develop in the tip of the plant.

Cordon tomatoes are trained upwards and supported by canes. Tie the stems to the canes at regular intervals, using soft string or raffia.

## Pinching out

This is the process whereby the growing tip is removed by hand to encourage the formation of side shoots or flower buds – and thus fruit. Runner beans, broad beans and tomatoes all benefit from this treatment.

Nip out the top buds once plants reach the required height, or for broad beans once they are in full flower (this also deters aphids). If you want runner bean plants to form a bush, pinch them out when 25 cm (10 in) high.

## Protecting

Check plants regularly for pests and diseases. Remove any pests, such as slugs or caterpillars, and any damaged growth as soon as it becomes apparent and treat where necessary (see 'Pests and Diseases' on pages 86 to 87 for more information). Another way to protect plants is to erect netting or other covers over plants to deter predators (see 'Protection' on pages 84 and 85).

## Weeding

Weeds are particularly prevalent during summer and you will need to check for them often, removing them as they occur to reduce competition for nutrients in the soil.

Hand weeding is usually recommended for vegetable gardens, but other methods may also be appropriate. For more information on weed control see page 89.

# Harvesting Vegetables and Herbs One of

the most rewarding aspects of gardening is to harvest produce from the plants that you have raised from seed and nurtured until they reach maturity. Shop-bought vegetables can never be as fresh – or taste so good.

## Vegetables

### Salad crops

Salad crops – whether lettuce, radish, beans or tomato – can be harvested throughout the summer. They should be picked as soon as they mature, so that they do not deteriorate. This is especially true of lettuces, which tend to bolt if left in the ground too long.

### Onions

These are ready for harvesting when the leaves start turning yellow and the tops keel over. You can speed up this process by bending the tops over by hand. Lift the bulbs gently with a fork and allow them to dry on a wire or wooden tray. Onions store well if they are hung in a cool, dry, frost-free place.

### Autumn cauliflowers

Harvest autumn cauliflowers from late summer until mid-winter, when the covering leaves start to open and reveal the curd beneath. Remove the curd by cutting through the main stem with a sharp knife; leave a row of leaves around the curd to protect it from damage while it is being handled.

### Podded vegetables

Where both the pod and its contents are to be eaten, start harvesting them once they are well-developed and the seeds are just visible as slight swellings along the pod. Where just the seeds are to be eaten, they must be allowed to develop and swell, but should be harvested before the pods change colour and the seeds become hard.

## Herbs

The best time to harvest herbs is mid-morning before the sun is too hot but after the dew has dried from the plants. Select the youngest and freshest leaves and shoots, discarding any with marks or blemishes.

### Herbs with thick or evergreen leaves

These can be cut and tied into small bunches before being hung up to dry in a warm, dark place for up to three weeks. Once dry, rub the leaves off the stem and place them in storage jars.

### Herbs with soft leaves

These are difficult to preserve by drying, but many freeze well. Fill an ice-cube tray with chopped herbs and a little water, then freeze. You can add the cubes to food during cooking.

| Herbs for freezing | |
| --- | --- |
| Basil | Mint |
| Chervil | Parsley |
| Chives | Salad |
| Dill | burnet |
| Fennel | Tarragon |

# Using Trees and Shrubs in Containers

Growing trees and shrubs in containers is the ideal way for many gardeners to increase quickly the range of plants they grow, especially for those with only a little spare time as there is no major soil preparation to be done. Autumn and spring are the more usual times for planting, but if grown in a container trees and shrubs will happily establish themselves in the summer, which is particularly useful for those wanting to create an instant display.

## Advantages of containers

There are many advantages to growing plants in containers, especially for those with only a small garden, or even no garden at all. It can offer solutions to problems of space, soil and climate, or provide a simple means of filling an unexpected gap in a border. We usually think first of bedding plants as the planting material, but trees or shrubs combined with perennials and annuals create a permanent feature and a continual source of pleasure.

### Dealing with lack of space
Plants in containers can be used to add interest in a small garden, as they can be moved from one site to another and so help to vary the seasonal display. The use of containers is also a very effective way of restricting the growth or spread of very vigorous plants.

### Gardens with no soil
It is quite feasible to grow plants outdoors without having a garden. Plants can easily be grown in containers and positioned on a terrace or balcony. Bay trees and thyme make excellent pot-grown herbs.

### Adapting to different climates
In more northerly districts or areas that are susceptible to late spring frosts, the growth rate of plants can be limited. By using containers, the plants can be moved to a more sheltered site or even taken indoors at certain times. This is particularly useful for pot-grown citrus fruits, such as lemons, which prefer to be overwintered under glass.

### Different soil types
Some plants thrive only in certain soil conditions, but there are limits to how much you can modify the soil in your garden to suit. In some gardens the soil has a high lime content, which is difficult and expensive to adjust. This makes growing plants that need acid soil, such as rhododendrons and camellias, impossible. The easy answer to this problem is to grow the plants you want in a container, in a specially formulated compost.

# Choosing containers

Purpose-made containers are available in a wide variety of shapes, sizes and materials, including concrete, clay, plastic and wood. Alternatively, you can make your own, either from scratch or by giving a new lease of life to an object that started as something completely different (see the project on page 90).

### Size and shape
While the final selection of a container may be down to personal choice, there are some practical considerations to be taken into account. Tall plants and climbing plants may need some form of support if they are to keep growing well. In this situation the dimensions of the container are particularly important; a deep container is necessary so that a stake or cane can be driven into the compost. Also the shape of the container will have a bearing on how rapidly the compost will dry out. One with a narrow base and wide top exposes a large surface area of compost to the atmosphere, and will therefore dry out more quickly than one with a narrow top.

### Porous materials
Containers made from a porous material, such as terracotta or wood, often lose a good deal of water through their sides due to evaporation. To a large extent, this loss can be avoided by lining the inner walls of the container with plastic sheeting before potting begins. Do not line the base of the container as this may impede drainage and cause the compost to become waterlogged.

## Trees and shrubs suitable for growing in containers

### Climbers and wall shrubs

*Actinidia kolomikta*

*Campsis × tagliabuana*

*Ceanothus* cultivars

*Clematis viticella* cultivars

*Euonymus fortunei* cultivars

*Jasminum nudiflorum*

*Lonicera × heckrottii*

*Vitis*

*Wisteria sinensis* cultivars
  (as a standard)

Pinus mugo *'Winter Gold'*

### Conifers

*Abies koreana*

*Cryptomeria japonica*

*Cupressus macrocarpa* cultivars

*Juniperus scopulorum* 'Skyrocket'

*Picea abies* 'Nidiformis'

*Pinus mugo*

*Taxus baccata*

*Thuja occidentalis* cultivars

Berberis

### Deciduous trees and shrubs

*Acer palmatum*

*Berberis thunbergii* cultivars

*Buddleja alternifolia*

*Davidia involucrata*

*Eucalyptus gunnii*

*Fuchsia magellanica*

*Magnolia stellata*

*Philadelphus* 'Belle Etoile'

*Spiraea japonica*

*Viburnum carlesii*

### Evergreen trees and shrubs

*Brachyglottis (Senecio)* 'Sunshine'

*Buxus sempervirens* cultivars

*Camellia*

*Cordyline australis*

*Escallonia* 'Slieve Donard'

*Eucalyptus*

*Laurus nobilis*

*Lavandula angustifolia*

*Mahonia aquifolium*

*Yucca filamentosa*

Buxus

# A Shrub Border for Year-round Interest

Summer offers the perfect opportunity to make plans for your border, as you sit back and reflect on its present appearance and how you might like to change or improve it. Take inspiration from friends and neighbours and visit as many show gardens as you can, so that you can design the border now, in preparation for planting in the autumn. When choosing plants for a shrub border there are a number of factors to consider: the size and shape of the shrub, which colours and forms complement one another, the suitability of a plant for a certain site, and whether or not it grows well in your type of soil.

## Planning the border

Perhaps one of the most interesting challenges for any gardener is to create a shrub border that will offer something of interest throughout the year. This is not simply a matter of selecting a range of shrubs that flower at different times; it also involves siting individual plants so that they draw the eye to various parts of the border.

### Creating seasonal interest
One of the best ways to draw attention deep into a border is to plant winter-flowering subjects at the rear, behind deciduous plants. The winter flowers can be seen through the deciduous shrubs, which will have no leaves on them at this time of year, but from mid-spring until mid-autumn, when winter-flowering shrubs tend to be relatively uninteresting, the foliage of the deciduous plants will hide them from view.

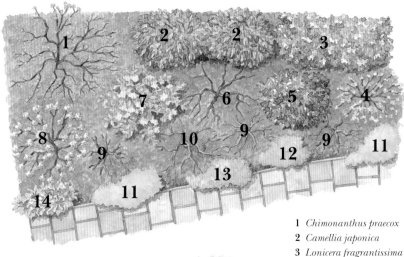

### Using scented plants
Siting scented shrubs close to pathways allows anyone passing by to appreciate their fragrance, whether it comes from the flowers, or from aromatic foliage. Even if the shrub does not have a strong shape or spectacular colour, its scent will add an extra delightful dimension to the border.

1  *Chimonanthus praecox*
2  *Camellia japonica*
3  *Lonicera fragrantissima*
4  *Abeliophyllum distichum*
5  *Choisya ternata*
6  *Hydrangea macrophylla*
7  *Mahonia aquifolium* 'Apollo'
8  *Viburnum × bodnantense* 'Dawn'
9  Shrub rose
10  *Paeonia officinalis*
11  *Lavandula* 'Hidcote'
12  *Rosmarinus officinalis*
13  *Santolina pinnata* subsp. *neapolitana*
14  *Salvia officinalis*

# Planting for year-round interest

## Spring

The new season is heralded by many small blooms in shades of cream, pink, white and yellow. They are often highly visible, due to the lack of foliage so early in the year, and many are scented. Later on, more colour is provided by the newly opening leaves.

Magnolia × soulangeana

| Plants with good flower colour | Plants with good foliage colour |
|---|---|
| *Daphne tangutica* Retusa Group | *Acer negundo* 'Flamingo' |
| *Hamamelis mollis* cultivars | *Berberis thunbergii* |
| *Kerria japonica* 'Pleniflora' | 'Atropurpurea Nana' |
| *Magnolia × soulangeana* | *Elaeagnus* 'Gilt Edge' |
| *Mahonia × media* 'Charity' | *Mahonia fremontii* |
| *Viburnum* | *Pieris* 'Forest Flame' |

## Summer

There is a huge choice of flowering shrubs for summer, and the plants can be combined to form a continuous display. Bear in mind that other colourful plants may offer stiff competition at this time, and interest can easily be diverted away from the shrub border.

Catalpa bignonioides *'Aurea'*

| Plants with good flower colour | Plants with good foliage colour |
|---|---|
| *Buddleja fallowiana* | *Berberis thunbergii* 'Rose Glow' |
| *Calycanthus occidentalis* | *Catalpa bignonioides* 'Aurea' |
| *Cistus ladinifer* | *Cornus alternifolia* 'Argentea' |
| *Embothrium coccineum* | *Luma apiculata* 'Glanleam Gold' |
| *Rosa* 'Blanc Double | *Physocarpus opulifolius* 'Diabolo' |
| de Coubert' | *Pyracantha* 'Mohave Silver' |

## Autumn

A large number of shrubs grown for their spring or summer flowers provide a second season of interest in autumn. This is when many of the deciduous shrubs really come to the fore, with their dramatic displays of changing leaf colours. Many others produce attractive fruits, often remaining on the branches through winter and into spring.

| Plants with good flower colour | Plants with good foliage colour | Plants with good fruit colour |
|---|---|---|
| *Ceanothus* 'Burkwoodii' | *Acer palmatum* | *Cotoneaster* 'Rothschildianus' |
| *Clerodendrum trichotomum* | *Cercidiphyllum japonicum* | *Pyracantha* cultivars |
| *Convolvulus cneorum* | *Cercis canadensis* | *Rosa rugosa* |
| *Hibiscus syriacus* | *Hydrangea quercifolia* | *Symphoricarpos orbiculatus* |

## Winter

Conifers and broad-leaved evergreens take centre stage in winter, their attractive foliage often contrasting with orange, red and yellow berries. There are also flowers at this time of year, with yellow predominating, and deciduous shrubs with brightly coloured stems.

Cornus alba

| Plants with good flower colour | Plants with good stem colour |
|---|---|
| *Chimonanthus praecox* | *Cornus alba* |
| *Garrya elliptica* | *Cornus stolonifera* |
| *Jasminum nudiflorum* | *Kerria japonica* |
| *Mahonia napaulensis* | *Leycesteria formosa* |
| *Rhododendron mucronulatum* | *Rubus thibetanus* |
| *Viburnum × bodnantense* | *Salix sachalinensis* 'Sekka' |

# summer bedding

The whole idea of summer bedding is to create a loud, bold display to reflect the brightest, warmest season of the gardening year. With the help of a good seed catalogue it is remarkably easy to create a flower bed that will provide colour and interest all summer long. No special growing facilities are required. The main display can be produced from hardy annuals sown directly into the border in mid- to late spring, or early summer in colder areas. More tender plants, such as half-hardy annuals, can be grown from seeds or cuttings raised on the kitchen windowsill.

## *materials & equipment*

*garden rake and trowel*

*high-phosphate fertilizer*

*sand*

*plastic bottle*

*stakes and twine*

### KEY TO PLANTING SCHEME *(see opposite)*

1  *Solenostemon (Coleus) blumei*
   (red-leaved form)
2  *Solenostemon (Coleus) blumei*
   (cream-leaved form)
3  *Cosmos*
4  *Coreopsis*
5  *Gomphrena*

6  *Zinnia elegans*
7  *Gaillardia × grandiflora* 'Kobold'
8  *Verbena bonariensis*
9  *Argyranthemum*
10 *Salvia viridis* 'Claryssa'
11 *Dahlia* (Collarette Series)
12 *Achillea ptarmatica*

## Transplanting the half-hardy annuals

**7** You can now add the more tender plants
that you have raised from seed indoors (alternatively you can buy these as 'starter plants'
from a garden centre). Start by digging a hole
slightly larger than the plant's root system.
Remove the young plant from its container
and, holding the plant by its root ball, place it
in the hole so that it sits firmly on the bottom.

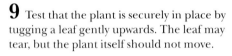

**8** Using the trowel pull the soil back into the
hole around the plant, and firm gently into
place. Immediately after planting, water
around the base of the plant.

**9** Test that the plant is securely in place by
tugging a leaf gently upwards. The leaf may
tear, but the plant itself should not move.

**10** As the bed comes into flower, fill any
gaps with half-hardy annuals, or use dwarf
annual climbers such as sweet peas to cover
the ground. Regular dead-heading will keep
the display flowering for as long as possible.

## Preparing the bed

**1** The bed can be marked out into planned blocks before sowing any seeds.

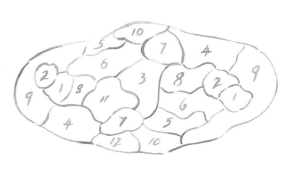

**2** Prepare the ground thoroughly to give the seedlings a good start, and rake the soil down to a fairly fine tilth, adding a high phosphate fertilizer at 30 grams per square metre (1 ounce per square yard), to encourage rapid root development.

**3** The easiest way to mark out the bed is to use dry sand. Slowly pour the sand out of a plastic bottle, forming narrow lines to indicate the intended margins of each group of plants. This will give a clear guide to where to sow or plant each group. If the sizes of the blocks are not quite right, you can rake the sand into the soil and mark out the border again.

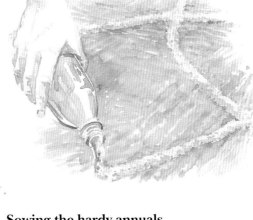

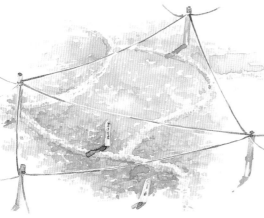

## Sowing the hardy annuals

**4** Sow the seeds into their respective segments, covering them lightly with soil to prevent them drying out. Label each group clearly. Provide protection from birds if necessary by stringing lengths of fine twine between short stakes.

**5** At this stage, some segments should be left empty, with no seed sown in them. These accommodate the more tender half-hardy annuals when they are planted out.

**6** When the seedlings emerge, gradually thin them out, to give them plenty of room to grow.

# propagation

*The rewards of gardening become plain for everyone to see in the summer as plants of all shapes and sizes push most of their energies into producing flowers. But, of all garden activities, few are more satisfying than raising plants yourself.*

*There are many different ways of propagating plants, and the summer is often the ideal season in which to do this. Growth is rapid at this time, which means that cuttings taken from stems or branches will readily take root. Seed heads form as flowers mature and these can be collected and stored to provide blooms for the following year. Bulbs and some other early flowering plants that have died down after a spring display can also be propagated now, to produce lots of strong, healthy new plants.*

# Cuttings With the higher temperatures and the long hours of day-

light, many plants have a surge of growth in summer and can be propagated by softwood cuttings well into the season. As this growth starts to harden and gradually matures it becomes semi-ripe; this stage of development is ideal for taking cuttings of many plants, including broad-leaved evergreens and some conifers. It is important to use only the best plants for propagation: the cuttings will be put under severe stress until they have rooted, and poor cuttings from poor plants will only deteriorate – they never improve.

## Semi-ripe cuttings

When collecting semi-ripe cuttings, choose only strong, vigorous shoots of the current season's growth. Do not select any thin or weak shoots, as these tend to be soft and sappy and usually rot. Discard any shoots showing signs of pests and disease.

**1** Remove the shoots with secateurs and place in a polythene bag with a little water to slow down wilting. Keep the bag closed but not sealed. Leave in a shady place if the cuttings are not to be potted up immediately.

**2** There are two types of semi-ripe cutting, nodal and heel, the latter being more effective when propagating evergreens.

### Nodal cuttings
If the shoot is more than 20 cm (8 in) long, reduce it to 10 to 12 cm (4 to 5 in) by making a cut straight across the stem with a sharp knife, 3 mm (⅛in) below a node or leaf joint. The positioning of the cut is important: the bark at the base of the cutting should be a light brown colour, indicating that the semi-ripe wood is forming.

### Heel cuttings
Pull a side shoot away from the main shoot, tearing it off with a strip of older wood (a heel) attached. The large wound stimulates root formation at the base of the cutting.

**3** Strip away all leaves from the bottom third of the cutting. If you leave them in place, they will rot in the compost and encourage the cutting itself to rot.

**4** Dip the cuttings into a hormone rooting powder, to speed root formation. Treat only the exposed woody surface at the base of the cutting; if the hormone powder comes into contact with soft juvenile bark, it may cause the cutting to rot. Tap off any excess powder.

**5** Insert the cuttings in a tray or pot of free-draining compost, or root them in a cold frame, planting the bottom third of the stem.

**6** Water the cuttings gently to settle the compost. They may appear loose and floppy for a few days but they should soon recover.

**7** Write the name of the plant and the date of propagation on a label and insert it in the container or cold frame. Place pots or trays in a shaded, damp environment; keep the top of the cold frame shaded in very sunny weather. Check the compost regularly to ensure it does not dry out. Covering the cuttings with clear plastic will speed up callus development and root formation.

## Plants that can be increased by semi-ripe cuttings in summer

| **Climbers** | **Conifers** | **Shrubs** |
|---|---|---|
| *Akebia quinata* | *Chamaecyparis* | *Berberis* (deciduous) |
| *Fremontodendron* | × *Cupressocyparis* | *Callicarpa bodinieri* |
| *Hedera* | *Cupressus* | *Ceanothus* (evergreen) |
| *Humulus lupulus* 'Aureus' | *Juniperus* | *Choisya ternata* |
| *Jasminum nudiflorum* | *Taxus* | *Escallonia* 'Iveyi' |
| *Passiflora* | *Thuja* | *Hydrangea* |
| *Trachelospermum* | *Thujopsis* | *Photinia* 'Birmingham' |
| *Wisteria* | *Tsuga* | *Viburnum carlesii* |

Passiflora caerulea

Thuja orientalis

Hydrangea *'Blue Wave'*

# Collecting Seeds and Bulbs

Although it is very convenient to buy seeds or bulbs in packets or bags, it is a relatively simple task – and much more satisfying – to collect them yourself from your own plants, or from those of a friend or neighbour. In some cases, especially with certain modern cultivars, plants raised from seed will not be exactly the same as the parent – but this can be part of the fun.

## Collecting seeds

With many plants, the seeds can be collected as they ripen, but before they are dispersed from the fruit. It is much easier to pick the seed heads a day or two early and get all of the seed in one place; if you wait too long, you will find yourself having to pick up seeds from the ground, one by one. Observation is the key, because often the seed will mature before the fruit starts to split open. Once the pods begin to turn brown and you see the first signs of a split in the casing, the seed head and its contents can be collected.

### Seed storage

**1** Collect the seed heads complete with stalks, and remove any leaves or remaining petals. Place bunches of stalks, seed head first, into paper bags, and tie the neck with string. Label the bags.

**2** Hang the bags in a cool, dry place. Shake them occasionally to release the seed. For smaller plants, lay the seed heads on trays lined with newspaper until the seed heads split open.

**3** Carefully remove the seed heads and stalks from the paper bags or trays. Hold the seed heads over sheets of paper and shake them until the seed falls out. Sift through with your fingers to clean out any bits of stalk or rubbish.

**4** Place the cleaned seed into dry envelopes or other paper packets (not plastic bags) and seal them up. Always take care to label the envelopes clearly, with the plant name and variety, the flower colour (if appropriate), and the date.

**5** Place the envelopes in a glass jar and seal the lid. Then put the jars in a cool, dry, dark place – this will make sure that the seed does not deteriorate.

If they are properly dried and kept in the correct conditions, the seeds of most vegetables and flowering plants will survive from two to five years in storage.

---

### Storage life of some seeds

| 1–2 years | 3–5 years | 5–10 years |
|---|---|---|
| *Callistephus chinensis* | *Capsicum* | *Calendula* |
| *Delphinium* | *Centaurea candidissima* | *Cosmos* |
| *Helichrysum monstrosus* | *Phlox drummondii* | *Eschscholzia* |
| *Iberis umbellata* | Tomato | *Nigella* |

# Collecting stem bulbils

Some species of lily produce embryo bulbs, called bulbils, in the angle of the leaf and flower stem (the 'leaf axil'). These can be collected and propagated to produce new plants that are identical to the parent. The bulbils are a dark green or blackish purple colour, and form through the spring and summer on the flower stem as it develops.

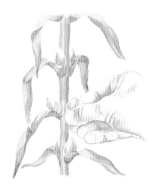 

**Lilies that produce stem bulbils**

*Lilium bulbiferum*
*Lilium lancifolium*
*Lilium sargentiae*
*Lilium sulphureum*

**1** The best time to collect stem bulbils is when they are ripe, about three weeks after the flowers have died down. Simply pick them from the stem by hand – they should come away quite easily.

**2** Sow the bulbils (just like seed) 2.5 cm (1 in) apart into trays of seed compost, so that they sit just below the surface. Now place the trays in a cold frame and leave them for a year.

The following autumn the young bulbs will be ready for planting out into a permanent site in the garden, although it will be a further two to three years before they produce any flowers.

# Creating bulbils

Other species of lily, particularly those that form their leaves either singly or in pairs on the flower stem, can be encouraged to produce bulbils. This method does involve sacrificing some of this season's flowers, but you will eventually get new plants in return.

**1** Choose a strong, healthy flower stem with several buds and cut it off at ground level just before the flowers open.

**2** Bury the stem in a tray of peat-based compost, leaving the top third of the stem exposed, and place the tray in a cold frame. Bulbils will usually form on the buried section of stem, producing roots to support themselves. At the same time, the flowering stem of the parent plant gradually withers and dies.

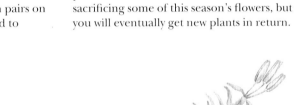

**Lilies that produce bulbils**

*Lilium duchartrei*
*Lilium formosanum*
*Lilium longiflorum*
*Lilium nepalense*
*Lilium pardalinum*
*Lilium wardii*

**3** The seed tray can then be emptied and the individual bulbils removed from the withered stem.

**4** Pot them into 5 cm (2 in) pots of peat-based compost, and put them in a cold frame for one year before planting them out.

# Division

Division is one of the simplest and easiest propagation methods for any keen gardener. As a basic technique, division involves separating one large plant into lots of smaller ones, or a number of small clumps, which are exact replicas of the parent plant. Although most plants are divided when they are dormant, there are some exceptions. Flag iris (*Iris germanica*) and some primula species establish better if they are divided and transplanted soon after flowering, in early summer. Because of the time of year, special care has to be taken to keep them cool and moist until they have formed new roots and established themselves in their new site.

## Simple division of fibrous-rooted plants

These plants often form a dense, over-crowded clump, which may become thick and matted with age. The performance of the clump will gradually deteriorate as those plants in the centre become old and unpro-ductive, often harbouring disease. With this type of plant, and particularly members of the primula family, the problem is often one of getting some leverage on the plant with-out causing it too much damage. The leaves may be relatively soft and fleshy, and any attempt to pull the plant apart with your bare hands often results in two handfuls of leaves and the clump remaining intact.

Persicaria bistorta *'Superba'*

Pulmonaria *'Blue Ensign'*

Epimedium × rubrum

**1** Once the plant has been lifted and the soil washed off, force the prongs of two garden forks into the centre of the clump so that they meet back to back. Apply pressure by levering the fork handles apart then pulling them together again until the clump starts to tease apart and splits in two.

**2** This process can be repeated again and again, until the clumps are of the desired size. Each time, aim to inflict as little damage on the plant as you can. Before replanting, check for any old, dead or diseased areas and cut them away with secateurs.

# Simple division of rhizomatous plants

Plants, such as the flag iris (*Iris germanica*), which have a thick fleshy modified stem or 'rhizome' spreading horizontally across the ground, can be propagated by cutting the rhizome into sections then replanting.

**1** Using a garden fork, dig up the plant, easing it out of the ground with as much root as possible. Wash the soil off the clump so that you can identify growth buds.

**2** Cut the thick fleshy stem or rhizome into pieces with a sharp knife, making sure each section has a growth bud.

**3** Check the rhizome pieces and discard any showing signs of decay or disease. Strip away any withered foliage, leaving four or five healthy leaves on each section. Trim these back to about 15 to 20 cm (6 to 8 in).

**4** Dig a shallow planting hole large enough to accommodate the rhizome's root system. Then, holding the rhizome by its leaves, lay it flat on the floor of the hole and gently spread out the roots.

**5** Pull the soil back into the hole around the plant and firm gently into place. Then water around the base of the plant to settle the soil and encourage the roots to grow.

# Division of bulbs

Many spring-flowering bulbs will have died down and become dormant so you can now lift any that you want to move to another site. Keep them clean and dry ready for replanting in autumn. Moving these bulbs also provides the opportunity to divide some of them and increase stocks. Some bulbs, such as the daffodil, produce the equivalent of side shoots, which form from buds close to the centre of the bulb. These 'side bulbs' grow on the parent bulb for two or three years before they eventually break off and become independent. See page 10 for techniques on lifting, dividing and storing bulbs.

Lilium lancifolium

Lilium martagon

---

**Bulbs that can be divided**

*Allium*
*Crinum*
Hyacinth (*Hyacinthus*)
Lily (*Lilium*)
Daffodil (*Narcissus*)
Snowdrop (*Galanthus*)
Tulip (*Tulipa*)

---

# Bulb Scaling

This technique is possibly the easiest method of propagation and is suitable for both lilies and fritillaria, the bulbs of which consist of clusters of scales attached to a basal plate. Very simply, the process involves encouraging the development of bulblets around the base of the scales; the bulblets can then be removed and potted up to form new plants.

## Simple scaling

**1** In late summer after flowering, as the stem begins to turn brown and dry, lift the bulbs from the ground and lay them in a seed tray to dry for two or three days. Then gently brush the soil from the outer scales of each bulb and remove the dead flower stem.

**2** Detach the outer scales from the bulb by breaking them off at the point where they join the basal plate. Up to 80 per cent of the outer scales can be removed from the parent bulb, which will still grow if it is replanted.

**3** Place the scales into a polythene bag and add fine grade, moist sphagnum moss peat, so that the bag contains equal proportions of peat and scales. Then add a small amount of fungicide, close the top, and turn the bag over several times to mix the contents evenly. Label the bag with the name and date and put it in a warm, dark place, such as an airing cupboard, for two to three months.

**4** After this time each scale should have produced at least one small embryo bulb (there may be three or four). The bulblets will be about 6 mm (¼ in) long, with tiny white fibrous roots growing from the base.

**5** Plant each scale, complete with bulblets, in a small 8 cm (3 in) pot of compost, with just the tip of the old scale showing. Top dress with sand and place outdoors.

**6** As the weather becomes warmer in the spring, new grass-like leaves will appear through the compost, growing from the bulblets. In the autumn these young bulbs can be planted in the garden soil and may flower the following year.

# Twin scaling

Twin scaling is a modification of scaling often used on daffodils and narcissi. Its advantage is that it produces many more plants from a single bulb, although the bulb is destroyed in the process and it does take longer for the new bulbs to reach flowering size.

**1** Lift the dormant bulbs in mid-summer, and lay them in a seed tray to dry for two or three days, before brushing the soil from the bulbs and removing the dead, dried roots.

**2** Trim the top of the bulbs and peel away the outer brown scales from each one.

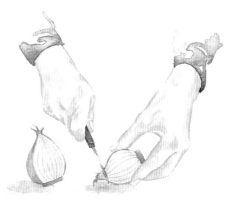

**3** Using a clean, sharp knife, cut the bulb into eight equal segments. Cut from top to bottom, and make sure that each segment has a piece of the bulb's basal plate attached.

**4** Divide each segment into pairs of scales by peeling apart the layers and cutting them off, again making sure they have a piece of basal plate attached. Each segment should provide three or four twin scale sections.

**5** Soak the twin scales in a fungicide solution for 10 minutes, then leave them to drain on a wire rack for a further 10 minutes.

**6** Place the twin scales in a polythene bag containing moist vermiculite (equal parts vermiculite and bulb scales) and mix them together. Blow air into the bag then seal it, before tying on a label with the plant's name and the date of propagation. Put the bag in a warm dark place for 12 to 14 weeks, turning it occasionally to keep the air moving.

**7** By now, each twin scale should have formed at least one bulblet. Plant them into 5 cm (2 in) pots of compost then place them in a heated frame or greenhouse.

**8** In spring the bulblets will produce grass-like leaves. As these die down, remove the bulblets from the scales. Repot in 5 cm (2 in) pots and place in a cold frame. After another year the young bulbs can be planted in the garden; they may flower three years later.

# Layering
As a method of increasing plant numbers, layering has certain advantages over rooting new plants from cuttings. It is a good propagation method for beginners as the stem will not die if the layering does not work first time and the technique can be tried again on the same stem. Also, although fewer plants are produced from layering, all of them will be much larger than newly rooted cuttings. The only drawback is that some plants take up to one and a half years to form self-supporting roots.

## Timing and methods

The method of layering will depend on the plant to be propagated. Size, shape and habit are important when considering the appropriate treatment. Serpentine layering, for instance, would not be suitable for stiff branches that might break if they were lowered to ground level. Although most plants are layered in the spring, some prefer to be treated in the summer, after flowering or when their stems are fully developed.

## Simple layering

This method is suitable for non-woody plants, such as border carnations, and should be carried out just after they have finished flowering. New roots will quickly form, after six to eight weeks. For best results, choose vigorous shoots that have not flowered.

**1** Select strong, healthy shoots that are young and flexible and, leaving them attached to the plant, remove most of the foliage. There should be only five to seven leaves at the growing tip of each shoot.

**2** Wound the stem by making a diagonal cut half way through it with a sharp knife and carefully prise open the cut.

**3** Make a shallow hole about 5 cm (2 in) deep in the soil and press the stem into it, with the wounding cut remaining open.

**4** Form a staple out of a piece of wire and use it to peg the stem into the bottom of the hole. Then fill the hole with soil, making sure the stem is covered, and water thoroughly.

**5** Once the wounded part of the stem has formed roots, it will start to grow more vigorously. Sever the stem so that the new plant is no longer attached to its parent, dig it up and plant it into its new flowering position.

# Serpentine Layering

For vigorous plants with long pliable stems, you can use a method of layering that will produce several new plants from the same stem, rather than just one as with simple layering. Sepentine layering should be carried out in the late summer when the shoots have reached their maximum length and the wood is mature, but still supple enough to bend into position. This method of propagation is suitable for plants such as clematis and wisteria, but it will be a whole year before the new plants can be separated from the parent.

**1** Select a long shoot and bend it down to the ground, marking the point where the first section of stem is to be buried; this should coincide with a bud and leaf joint.

**2** Dig a shallow hole, about 8 to 10 cm (3 to 4 in) deep, where the stem is to be buried; shape it so that it has a shallow slope on the side nearest to the parent plant and a steep slope on the opposite side.

**3** Wound the stem with a sharp knife, making a shallow cut just behind the bud.

**4** Form a staple out of wire and use it to peg the stem securely into the bottom of the hole. Return the soil to the hole to cover the stem and firm it gently in place.

**5** Leave the next length of stem, with two or three leaves, above ground. Bend down the next section and repeat steps 1 to 4. This can be done several times until about 45 cm (18 in) of stem remains at the shoot tip.

The following year the layered sections of stem should have rooted and started producing shoots. They can now be dug up and moved, after leaf fall in the autumn, but take great care not to damage the new roots.

# Natural layering

Some plants are helpful enough to layer themselves naturally and really need only a little help or encouragement to produce lots of new plants. Strawberries in particular produce new plants on horizontal stems called runners, soon after flowering has finished.

**1** Dig a hole beneath the new plant forming on the runner and plunge an 8 cm (3 in) pot of soil or compost into the ground. Peg the runner and new plant into the pot.

**2** After about six weeks this new plant will have rooted and will be growing more strongly, so can then be separated from the parent plant. Cut through the runner, lift the pot from the soil, and replant in a new site.

# seasonal pruning

*It is very easy to dismiss pruning as a winter task, and for some plants winter is the main season for pruning, but for many others summer is the most appropriate time. Pruning includes the shaping and training of young plants,*  *particularly those that must be clipped or trimmed into a pre-determined shape or pattern, such as for topiary or formal hedges. Techniques used to control the growth habit of plants, such as training fruit trees into fans or espaliers, make it possible to grow them in a relatively confined space. Other forms of summer pruning include removing old, faded flowers, and stopping or pinching out the tip of a plant to form a large single bloom or a multi-stemmed plant with many clusters of small flowers.*

# The Essentials

It is important to use the right equipment for your particular pruning job, to be sure of getting the best results. When pruning, never attempt to cut through wood that is too thick for the tools you are using as this will only wrench the tools and spoil the cutting action, as well as probably damaging the branch being cut. It will also put severe strain on your wrists and arms, as it forces you to apply excessive pressure.

## Secateurs

The best tool for most types of pruning is a pair of sharp secateurs and there are many different kinds available. Check them before

### The anvil type
The anvil type of secateurs has a single straight-edged cutting blade, which closes down onto a block of softer metal.

you buy to make sure the grip is comfortable. Most models now feature a safety catch, to keep the blades closed when not in use.

### The ratchet type
A useful modification allows these secateurs to cut through a shoot or branch in gradual stages. As they require less effort, these are ideal for gardeners with a small hand span, and are very good for reducing fatigue.

### The blade and half-anvil type
This is the type of secateur most commonly used. As with the similar parrot-bill type, these have a bypass or scissor-like cutting action, in which one convex cutting blade cuts past a second, fixed curved bar.

## Long-handled pruners

Also known as 'loppers', these are basically secateurs with long handles which provide extra leverage to cut thicker wood.

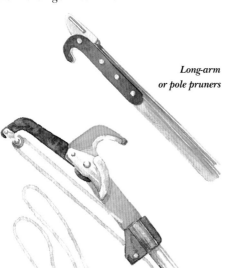

*Long-arm or pole pruners*

## Long-arm pruners

These consist of a pole 2 to 3 m (6 to 9 ft) long with a hooked anvil and curved blade at the tip, the blade being operated by a lever at the opposite end. They are capable of cutting through branches up to 3 cm (1¼ in) thick. These pruners are used to extend the reach when pruning high tree branches. Models with a small basket attached close to the blade are now available, and these are recommended for picking fruit.

# Pruning saws

Saws are used for cutting large stems in small spaces or where the angle of the branch is narrow. Some pruning saws have a tapering blade and different sized teeth on each side, one set of teeth producing a smoother finished cut than the other. Others have a curved blade tapered to a sharp point and sloping teeth designed to cut on the pull stroke, which is very useful in a confined space. Many of the modern saws are designed to fold, with the blade closing into the handle when not in use.

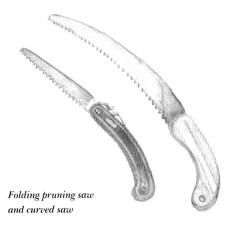

*Folding pruning saw and curved saw*

# Hand shears

Used mainly for hedge clipping, hand shears come with straight blades, each with a deep notch at the base for cutting thicker stems. Choose a good-quality pair as the cutting edge will stay sharp longer. If a large amount of hedge clipping is to be done, a powered hedge trimmer with reciprocating blade is a worthwhile addition to the tool shed.

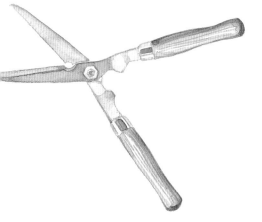

# Pruning knives

Although a sharp general-purpose knife will cope adequately with many tasks, a specialist pruning knife will be more effective. It has a slightly larger, curved blade, which makes it easier to cut through thicker branches.

*Ordinary and curved blades*

# Principles of pruning

There are three main categories of pruning, each with a different purpose. Formative pruning, carried out when the plant is young, is perhaps the most influential as it is used to develop a strong, balanced structural framework of stems and branches. The amount of pruning and training required depends on the type of plant, as well as the shape and effect you want to achieve. Routine pruning, carried out when the plant is well grown, may be variously used – to keep the plant within its allotted space, to maintain its health and vitality, or to induce it to produce flowers or fruit. Again, the techniques you use will vary according to the individual needs of your plant. The third main type is known as renovation pruning, a drastic treatment that may be necessary to restore old or neglected trees or shrubs. The first stage in any form of pruning is to remove all diseased, damaged, dying or dead wood. This enables you to assess the amount of live, healthy wood. Next you should prune out any thin, weak stems. It is then possible to decide which shoots should be cut back or removed to obtain a well-balanced plant.

**Pruning wounds**
Whenever a plant is pruned, there is the risk of rot developing within the pruning wound, attacking the plant and slowly killing it. Until recently it has been standard practice to cover such cuts with a wound paint, but research now indicates that wound paints are not very effective in controlling disease.

In fact, in some cases the paints may even encourage disease by sealing the spores of infectious organisms into new wounds. The surest way to prevent wound damage is to prune at the right time, when the plant is at its healthiest and therefore best able to recover quickly.

# Annuals
There are various techniques you can use to extend the growing season of the annuals in your garden, and so ensure a long and colourful display throughout the summer. These tasks involve removing dead growth and any overgrown or overcrowded stems, as well as supporting and training tall or slender stems that may bend if left to their own devices.

## Shoot thinning

This technique allows more air to flow through the plant, which in turn reduces the chances of mildew occurring. For well-established plants, thin out some of the shoots by removing them completely, cutting them off at the base, before pinching out the tips of the strongest shoots. Select the thinnest and weakest shoots for removal; or, if the shoots are of equal size but are over-crowded, remove about one third of them.

## Pinching out

To check the growth of plants that tend to become too tall and fall over, such as chrysanthemums and dahlias, create multi-branched stems by pinching out the growing point of each shoot. Do this when the shoots are about one third of their ultimate height, and at least a month before they are due to flower. In mid-summer, remove the top 10 cm (4 in) of the most dominant shoots. This may delay flowering by a couple of weeks, but will not affect the length of the flowering period and will encourage more flowers to develop. It may, however, reduce the ultimate height of the plants by a quarter.

## Supporting stems

In addition to shoot thinning and pinching out shoot tips, many plants will also benefit from being provided with some form of support. Twigs or stakes should be positioned before the top growth is 15 cm (6 in) high, as this encourages the plant to grow up or through the support, disguising it in the process. If left unsupported for too long, the plant may fall over and there is a danger of the stems becoming bent and kinked.

**Supporting sweet peas**
To get plenty of really large blooms, sweet peas need to be grown up sticks or canes as cordons, with the plants being tied to the supports at 20 cm (8 in) intervals. Although climbing sweet peas normally support themselves by means of leaf tendrils, which curl around the canes, this self-clinging uses up a lot of energy. To encourage the plant to channel its resources into the production of flowers, it is better to remove the tendrils as soon as they appear, and to tie the stems to the support with soft string.

# Dead-heading

Both hardy and half-hardy annuals will need to be regularly dead-headed throughout the summer months in order to keep them flowering for as long as possible and to remove unsightly blooms. Cutting off the dying flowerheads before the seed has developed will stimulate the plant to throw up more flowers, in a determined attempt to produce the seed that will ensure the plant's survival the following year.

| Flowers for dead-heading | | |
|---|---|---|
| *Achillea* | *Gaillardia* | Scabious (*Scabiosa*) |
| *Anthemis* | *Oenothera* | *Sidalcea* |
| *Dahlia* | Peony (*Paeonia* ) | Sweet pea (*Lathyrus odoratus*) |

Clematis *'Lasurstern'*

Paeonia lactiflora

*Sweet pea*

# Disbudding

If blooms with long clean stems are required, some of the stems can be disbudded. Keep the top 'primary' bud and remove the two smaller 'secondary' buds. This technique will produce fewer, larger blooms, which are ideal as cut flowers. Alternatively, to increase the number of flowers produced, leave the two smaller 'secondary' buds on the stem and remove the top 'primary' bud. The flowers will be smaller, but they will create an excellent garden display throughout the summer.

# Cutting back

As soon as the blooms on the earlier-flowering plants, such as columbine (*Aquilegia*), foxglove (*Digitalis*), *Erigeron* and mulleins (*Verbascum*), have finished, cut down the flowering stems to leave about 8 cm (3 in) above soil level. Although this is unlikely to result in a further display of flowers, it should encourage the plant to produce a new flush of leaves, which will provide ground cover and help to suppress weeds for the rest of the summer.

# Shrubs
Almost all shrubs need pruning at some stage, be it formative, routine or renovation pruning. As summer is not the main time for planting shrubs, formative pruning is not necessary. Also, renovation pruning is best carried out in the dormant season, with one or two exceptions being left until spring. Summer pruning, therefore, is limited to routine pruning of flowering shrubs and those that would bleed if pruned at any other time.

## Pruning cuts

As with any type of pruning, at any time of year, the position of the cut is important in promoting healthy growth, in the right direction. For stems with alternate facing buds, the cut should be at an angle, about 2.5 mm (⅛ in) above a healthy bud, which will encourage rapid healing. For opposite facing buds, make the cut straight across.

## Routine pruning of flowering shrubs

Most flowering shrubs are best pruned soon after they have finished flowering. Many deciduous shrubs that flower in spring or early summer carry their flowers on wood produced the previous year and these will benefit from being tidied up in the summer.

**Shrubs with a naturally twiggy habit**
Shrubs such as *Chaenomeles* and forsythias that have a naturally twiggy habit with numerous crossing branches will need little pruning. They will, however, respond well to 'spur' pruning, which will encourage heavier flowering and prevent the shrub becoming too straggly; this is particularly important when they are grown as wall shrubs. 'Spur' pruning involves removing the tips of the main shoots – about 15 cm (6 in) or so – to encourage side shoots (laterals) to develop; these side shoots can be trimmed back to three to five leaves later on in the season.

**Dense, bushy shrubs**
Shrubs that produce shorter side shoots, such as *Deutzia*, *Philadelphus* and *Weigela*, will become a dense thicket of matted untidy growth if left unpruned, often becoming top heavy with crowded twiggy growth that will gradually produce fewer and fewer flowers. The best way to avoid this happening is to prune in mid-summer, immediately after the flowers have faded, cutting the old flower-bearing shoots back to within 5 to 8 cm (2 to 3 in) of ground level. This treatment will encourage the shrub to produce new flower-bearing shoots for the following year.

---

**Shrubs pruned in summer after flowering**

| | | |
|---|---|---|
| *Deutzia* | *Kerria* | *Rubus cockburnianus* |
| *Escallonia* | *Kolkwitzia* | *Spiraea* 'Arguta' |
| *Euphorbia* | *Lonicera × purpusii* | *Stephanandra* |
| *Fremontodendron* | *Philadelphus* | *Weigela florida* cultivars |

---

# Berries and fruits

Many shrubs that flower in the summer are pruned immediately after flowering. However there are exceptions – those that provide additional seasonal interests, such as attractive fruits and berries. These plants are often pruned in the late winter or early spring, by cutting back the previous season's growth in order to form flowering spurs.

---

**Shrubs left unpruned for display**

| | | |
|---|---|---|
| *Aronia* | *Cotoneaster* | *Pyracantha* |
| *Berberis* | *Hippophae* | *Rosa rugosa* |
| *Colutea* | *Ilex* | *Symphoricarpos* |

---

Pyracantha

Ilex

Rosa rugosa

# Sap bleeding

Although shrubs should ideally be pruned either after they have flowered or when they are dormant, some species will bleed large amounts of sap if pruned in the late winter or early spring. To prevent this happening, these shrubs should be pruned when they are in full leaf. Prune them in summer when they are growing rapidly and the leaves have expanded; as the leaves search for any available moisture, they will draw the sap from the pruning wounds, leaving them relatively dry so less susceptible to bleeding.

---

**Shrubs that bleed and need summer pruning**

| | | |
|---|---|---|
| *Acer japonica* | *Aesculus parviflora* | *Prunus* |
| *Acer palmatum* | *Magnolia stellata* | *Sophora* |

---

# Pinching out

This is a useful technique often used for shaping a plant or getting it to produce lots of side shoots or branches. It involves removing the tip or growing point of each shoot. If this is done when the growth is soft and sappy, no pruning equipment is required, as the shoot tips can be pinched out between finger and thumb. The trick is to pinch while the shrub is growing rapidly, then the wound will quickly heal.

# Climbers and Wall Shrubs

Summer pruning of climbers and wall shrubs helps to increase the production of flowers in the following year. It is also used to prevent plants becoming too large and unruly, especially where they are to be trained against a wall or fence.

## Supporting climbers

Natural climbers that are 'self-supporting' will need to be checked regularly and coaxed into growing in the desired direction; those such as twiners and scramblers may need fixing in place with ties until the tendrils or twining stems have attached themselves to the support. Tying-in is also a useful method of controlling the direction of growth. Older stems that are intended to be kept for a number of years should be re-tied annually when the climber or wall shrub is pruned, to prevent the ties strangling the stem.

## Routine pruning

Climbers and wall shrubs that flower on wood formed in the previous year should be pruned after flowering. This includes some evergreens and early-flowering clematis. First remove any dead or damaged wood, then cut back straggly shoots to retain the plant's shape. Tie in any long extension growths.

Wall shrubs grown for their ornamental fruits, such as cotoneaster, produce most of their new growth in mid-summer, after flowering. If left unpruned, these shoots will obscure the berries. In late summer, prune the new growths back to within 10 cm (4 in) of the main stem. These short shoots then form spurs that will bear next year's flowers.

### Climbers and wall shrubs for summer pruning

| | | |
|---|---|---|
| *Aristolochia* | *Clematis armandii* | *Hydrangea* |
| *Billardiera* | *Clematis montana* | *Parthenocissus* |
| *Campsis* | *Clerodendrum* | *Pyracantha* |
| *Ceanothus* | *Cotoneaster* | *Thunbergia* |
| *Chaenomeles* | *Escallonia* | *Wisteria* |

Wisteria

Clematis

Escallonia

# Wisteria

The vigorous habit of wisteria has put many gardeners off growing it, as they are unsure how to tackle the prolific growth in order to contain the stems and produce plenty of flowers. Provided pruning is carried out regularly, however, the task is fairly simple.

## Pruning methods

In order to give an overview of the life-cycle of wisteria, the illustrations below follow the pruning process from planting to maturity.

## On planting

Fix support wires to a fence or wall. Tie the main stem to a cane then cut it back to 75 to 90 cm (2½ to 3 ft). Remove any side shoots.

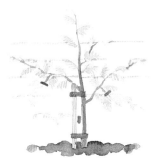

### First year – summer

Train long twining shoots into position to form a framework of branches. Cut back other shoots to 15 to 20 cm (6 to 8 in) to encourage flower-bearing spurs to form.

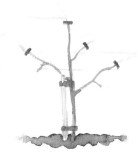

### First year – winter

In winter, cut back the leading shoot and the lateral or side shoots until just three buds remain on each one. This will help in the formation of strong new branches.

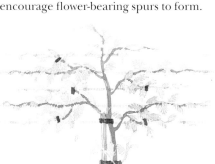

### Second year – summer

Pinch out the tip of the leading shoot to the required height and cut back thin, spindly side shoots, to encourage a bushy habit.

### Second year – winter

To encourage the formation of spurs, which will eventually produce flowers, cut back the new lateral growth to two or three buds.

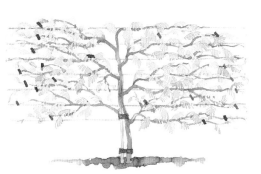

### Third and subsequent years – summer

By now only routine maintenance pruning will be needed. Keep the main framework branches in check by cutting back any over-long growths. Cut back the lateral growth to 15 cm (6 in) to encourage flowering spurs.

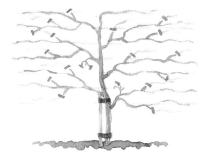

### Third and subsequent years – winter

Cut back the flowering spurs to just two or three buds. This will stimulate growth and ensure the climber flowers well the following season. Check the ties on the main stem each year and replace if necessary.

# Roses
Although most roses are generally pruned in the spring or autumn, there is one important exception: rambling roses, with their wild, vigorous habit and flexible stems, are best pruned in the summer, after they have flowered. There are also a number of other routine pruning tasks to be performed now, that are necessary to maintain the health of the other types of roses in your garden and keep them flowering well throughout the season.

## Rambling roses

These will flower quite satisfactorily for a number of years without any regular pruning, but they will eventually become a tangled mass of overcrowded unmanageable shoots, prone to attack by pests and diseases, if they are neglected completely. The best time to prune is in the late summer, after the single flush of flowers is over.

### Pruning cuts
As with all roses, use clean, sharp secateurs or a pruning knife to prevent ragged edges that are susceptible to invasion by pests and diseases. Make each cut at an angle, 5 mm (¼ in) from an outward facing bud, being sure to cut back into healthy white wood.

### Routine pruning
Start by removing any dead, damaged or diseased shoots, before cutting out about a quarter to a third of the oldest shoots; the aim is to leave only young vigorous stems that are no more than two years old. Any side shoots should be cut back to two or three buds, from which many of the next year's flowers will originate.

### Training
It is important to train the remaining shoots after pruning. The main stems are trained into a horizontal or near horizontal position; this will encourage the development of short flower-bearing lateral shoots along the length of the stem. Use ties to secure the new shoots to a supporting framework.

| Rambling roses |
| --- |
| *Rosa* 'Albertine' |
| *Rosa* 'Emily Gray' |
| *Rosa* 'Goldfinch' |
| *Rosa* 'Rambling Rector' |
| *Rosa* 'Sanders' White' |
| *Rosa* 'Silver Moon' |

Rosa *'Goldfinch'*

Rosa *'Sanders' White'*

Rosa *'Albertine'*

# General tasks

In order to keep all your roses growing and flowering well, or to improve their performance and the quality of the blooms, there are a number of tasks that should be tackled throughout the season, depending on the individual habit of your rose.

### Disbudding
This is a technique that can be used to create fewer, but larger blooms on a rose bush. With most hybrid roses, as the new flower-bearing stem develops, the cluster of blooms will consist of one central bud and a number of small lateral buds. Snap off these lateral buds while they are still soft and sappy so that all of the plant's energies will be directed into the one remaining bloom, creating a much larger individual flower.

### Dead-heading
After flowering, dead rose blooms may remain on the plant for several months and in this situation the plant will divert a good deal of energy into producing seed. Once this process starts, the plant gradually stops producing flowers altogether. A common mistake is to remove the flower with a length of stem bearing four or five leaves; removing the leaves is unnecessary and only a small section of stem, about 10 cm (4 in) long, should be cut off with the dead bloom.

### Sucker removal
A very important pruning task in the summer is removing suckers from roses. You can usually identify a sucker by its leaves. With most rose cultivars the leaf consists of 5 to 7 leaflets, but suckers have leaves with 7 to 11 leaflets, each ending with a sharp point, and they are usually a much paler green than those on the rest of the plant.

**1** Using a trowel, carefully dig the soil from around the base of the sucker, to the point where it is attached to the parent plant.

**2** Wearing a thick leather glove to protect your hand from the thorns, grip the sucker firmly, just above the point where it is growing from the root of the parent.

**3** Tear the sucker free from the parent plant and trim any loose bark on the parent with a sharp knife. Discard the sucker and replace the soil around the base of the plant.

Standard roses often produce suckers above ground, on the stem, in addition to those originating from the roots, and these may compete with the top growth and eventually take over. Wearing thick leather gloves, snap off the sucker growths where they are attached to the main stem or 'leg' of the plant. Do this while the suckers are still soft and sappy.

# Trees

Most trees will need pruning at some point in their life: initially for form and shape, then as a routine task to maintain balance and health, and as a means of renovating an old or neglected specimen. The majority of these tasks are carried out in the dormant season when trees often naturally prune themselves, or in the spring to correct misshapen or overgrown crowns. However, there are certain trees that can be pruned only in the summer and these include those that are susceptible to bleeding as well as deciduous trees that flower in spring or summer. It is also a good time to make general checks on all your trees and correct any problems that occur.

## Pruning cuts

It is important to make clean cuts when pruning trees as the pruning wounds are larger than, say, on a shrub, and so more susceptible to pests and diseases. Using sharp secateurs, make each cut at an angle, about 5 mm (¼ in) above a bud that faces the direction in which you want the new shoot to develop. Place the base of the thin blade of the secateurs near the bud for the best cut.

## General tasks

Apart from trees that must be pruned in the summer, most other trees will benefit from some general maintenance pruning at this time, to ensure they remain healthy for the rest of the growing season, and in preparation for pruning later in the year.

### Broad-leaved evergreens

Because of their size these trees are not a main feature in most domestic gardens. Pruning and training to establish their shape is carried out in the autumn when a strong main stem is established. During the summer, however, it is important to check for dead or dying branches and for any showing signs of damage or disease. Remove them before the problem spreads or causes more damage through falling branches or rough wounds that leave the tree open to infection.

On trees with variegated leaves, check carefully to see if any shoots have reverted, that is the leaves have become plain green again. The variegation is simply a mutation, so the leaves may revert to the original foliage at any time. Branches and leaves that have reverted are usually more vigorous, so they must be removed with secateurs as soon as they appear, otherwise the overall look of the tree will be spoiled.

## Conifers

Coniferous trees such as cypress, firs and pines tend to produce a single main stem with whorls of branches developing along it. Provided the main stem remains intact, the tree will grow naturally in a uniform and upright manner. The only pruning that needs to be done, at any time, is to remove dead, dying and diseased or damaged branches, and this can safely be carried out during the summer. It is important not to over prune: most conifers do not normally re-grow from mature wood as there are few or no dormant buds present in the older woody branches and stems.

## Deciduous trees

Many deciduous trees respond better to pruning either after they have finished flowering or when they are dormant, and this is usually in the autumn. However, trees that flower early, in the spring or at the beginning of the summer, need to be pruned before this, from the middle to the end of the summer, to give them as much time as possible to produce the new growth that will bear next year's flowers. Prune to correct the shape and remove any split or broken branches by making a straight cut below the damaged area.

## Deciduous trees that bleed

Other deciduous trees that are prone to bleeding are better pruned during this season, when they are in full leaf, to protect them from excessive loss of sap, which would considerably weaken the tree and may eventually contribute to its death. Once the leaves have fully expanded and matured, they will readily draw back the sap from the pruning wounds in an attempt to gather as much moisture as possible.

---

### Trees that bleed

Birch *(Betula)*
Cherry *(Prunus)*
Horse chestnut *(Aesculus)*
Maple *(Acer)*
*Sophora*
*Tilia*
Walnut *(Juglans)*

---

### Spring/Summer flowering trees

Chestnut *(Castanea)*
Chilean firebush *(Embothrium coccineum)*
Golden rain *(Laburnum)*
Judas tree *(Cercis siliquastrum)*
Redbud *(Cercis)*
*Robinia*

---

Acer palmatum

Betula pendula

Laburnum

# Fruit
While pruning fruit trees is usually seen as a winter task, pruning is often carried out in summer in order to encourage the trees to produce more fruit or, in the case of plums and their relatives, to avoid the risk of infection. Dwarf pyramid trees also need pruning in summer, to maintain their shape. For training new fruit trees, refer to the project on pages 58 to 60.

## Trained fruit trees

The standard method of summer pruning is called the 'Modified Lorette System'. It helps to maintain a constant supply of fruit buds, and suppresses vigorous shoot growth. It is carried out in late summer, once the young shoots have become woody at the base.

**1** All new lateral branches growing directly from the main stem or a main branch that are longer than 22 cm (9 in) should be cut back to three to five leaves above the basal cluster. Side shoots growing from spurs and existing laterals must be pruned back to just one leaf above the basal cluster of leaves. This job will continue throughout the late summer.

**2** To prevent secondary side shoots from developing below the earlier pruning cuts, leave a small number of longer shoots unpruned. These shoots will draw in sap and therefore discourage any secondary growth from developing. After the fruit has been harvested, in mid-autumn, prune back these 'sap-drawing shoots' to a single bud.

## Fruit susceptible to fungal disease

Plums, greengages, damsons and all relatives of the cherry are prone to a fungal disease called 'silver leaf' (*Chondrostereum purpureum*), the spores of which appear in the autumn and winter, entering the plant through pruning cuts. Cut back any affected growth in the summer to reduce the risk of the infection spreading.

## Maintaining the shape of dwarf fruit trees

The dwarf pyramid tree was developed for commercial growing of apples and pears but it is also ideal for small gardens. The shape saves space, with the upper branches being shorter than the lower ones, and the fruit is accessible, making harvest easier. The size and shape of the tree must, however, be maintained by regular pruning. Once it has reached the required height of about 2.5 m (8 ft), restrict the tree's growth by cutting back the main stem to one bud in the early summer each year. Throughout the summer, shorten shoots growing from main branches to leave just three leaves, and cut back side shoots growing from existing laterals to one leaf above the basal cluster of leaves.

# Repairing damaged branches

For fruit trees that produce an unexpectedly large crop, and for trees such as plums that often produce heavy crops, the sheer weight of the fruit may cause branches to break or split. These damaged branches must be pruned back or removed in the summer, to prevent any invasion of pests and diseases.

# Pruning soft fruits

Soft fruits, such as blackberries, loganberries and raspberries, which grow on canes, are pruned in the summer, after fruiting, to produce plenty of new growth for the following year. The canes also need to be trained on a post and wire support.

## Blackberries and loganberries

**1** As the new canes grow in the late spring and early summer, they are gathered up and loosely bunched together in the centre of the plant. This makes it much easier to pick the fruit, which grows on last year's canes.

**2** Immediately after harvest, cut down all of the old fruiting canes at the base of their stems, close to ground level.

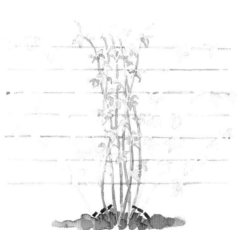

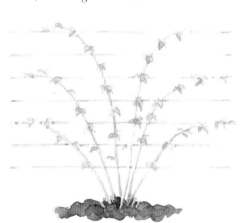

**3** Remove the ties from the bunch of young canes in the centre of the plant, carefully spread the canes out and train them along the wire supports, removing any canes that are surplus to your requirements. Leave a gap in the centre of the plant, into which the new canes can grow.

## Raspberries

**1** All of the fruited canes should be cut down to ground level immediately after harvest. Also remove any thin, weak or damaged canes, so that the shoots that remain are healthy and strong and are given as much growing room as possible.

**2** As the canes grow, loosely but securely attach the new shoots to the wire supports. spacing the canes regularly at 10 cm (4 in) intervals. To make sure that the canes have adequate growing space, cut out any excess canes and pull up any sucker growths that begin to encroach on to the pathway. When the canes reach the very top of the support, the tips must be pruned back to within 8 cm (3 in) of the wire.

# Hedges
Most hedges fall into two categories: formal and informal. Formal hedges require regular clipping to control their growth and retain a particular shape; this type makes an effective barrier or shelter or an elegant backdrop for other plants. Informal hedges require less pruning and are an excellent means of displaying plants that produce attractive flowers or fruits.

## When to prune

How and when the hedge is pruned depends largely on the type of shrub used. Generally the best time to prune is soon after flowering, removing only the flower-bearing shoots.

Plants, such as firethorn (*Pyracantha*) or *Rosa rugosa*, which produce attractive berries or hips after the flowers, should not be pruned until after the fruits have finished.

## Formal hedges

| Evergreen hedges | Best height | Clipping times |
|---|---|---|
| Box (*Buxus sempervirens*) | 30–60 cm (1–2 ft) | *3 x but not in winter* |
| *Elaeagnus × ebbingei* | 1.5–3.0m (5–10 ft) | *1 x mid- to late summer* |
| *Escallonia* | 1.2–2.5m (4–8 ft) | *1 x after flowering* |
| Firethorn (*Pyracantha*) | 2.0–3.0m (6½–10 ft) | *2 x after flowering & in autumn but avoid berries* |
| *Griselinia littoralis* | 1.2–3.0m (4–10 ft) | *2 x late spring/summer* |
| Holly (*Ilex aquifolium*) | 2.0–4.0m (6½–13 ft) | *1 x late summer* |
| Laurel (*Prunus laurocerasus*) | 1.2–3.0m (4–10 ft) | *1 x mid to late summer* |
| Leyland cypress (× *Cupressocyparis leylandii*) | 2.0–6.0m (6½–20 ft) | *3 x but not in winter* |
| *Lonicera nitida* | 0.9–1.2m (3–4 ft) | *3 x but not in winter* |
| Privet (*Ligustrum*) | 1.5–3.0m (5–10 ft) | *3 x but not in winter* |
| Western red cedar (*Thuja plicata*) | 1.5–4.0m (5–13 ft) | *2 x spring/early autumn* |
| Yew (*Taxus baccata*) | 1.2–6.0m (4–20 ft) | *2 x summer/autumn* |
| **Deciduous hedges** | | |
| Barberry (*Berberis thunbergii*) | 0.6–1.2m (2–4 ft) | *1 x in summer* |
| Beech (*Fagus sylvatica*) | 1.5–6.0m (5–20 ft) | *1 x late summer* |
| Hawthorn (*Crataegus monogyna*) | 1.5–3.0m (5–10 ft) | *2 x summer/autumn* |
| Hornbeam (*Carpinus betulus*) | 1.5–6.0m (5–20 ft) | *1 x late summer* |

## Informal hedges

| Evergreen hedges | Best height | Clipping times |
|---|---|---|
| Barberry (*Berberis darwinii*) | 1.5–2.5m (5–8 ft) | *1 x after flowering* |
| Cotoneaster (*Cotoneaster lacteus*) | 1.5–2.2m (5–7 ft) | *1 x after fruiting* |
| Firethorn (*Pyracantha*) | 2.0–3.0m (6½–10 ft) | *2 x after flowering & in autumn but avoid berries* |
| Holly (*Ilex aquifolium*) | 2.0–4.0m (6½–13 ft) | *1 x late summer* |
| Lavender (*Lavandula*) | 0.5–1.0m (20–39 in) | *2 x spring/after flowering* |
| Tassel bush (*Garrya elliptica*) | 1.5–2.2m (5–7 ft) | *1 x after flowering* |
| *Viburnum tinus* | 1.0–2.5m (3–8 ft) | *1 x after flowering* |
| **Deciduous hedges** | | |
| Barberry (*Berberis thunbergii*) | 0.6–1.2m (2–4 ft) | *1 x after flowering* |
| *Forsythia × intermedia* | 1.5–2.5m (5–8 ft) | *1 x after flowering* |
| Hawthorn (*Crataegus monogyna*) | 1.5–3.0m (5–10 ft) | *1 x winter* |
| *Rosa rugosa* | 1.0–1.5m (3–5 ft) | *1 x after flowering* |

# Maintenance pruning

The aim of clipping is to produce a hedge of the desired size which is evenly covered with growth over its entire surface. The average hedge need not exceed 75 cm (2½ft) in width (this applies to even the most vigorous species of hedge plants), provided it is pruned and trimmed correctly in the early stages of development. Formal hedges should always be narrower at the top than at the base, to make trimming easier.

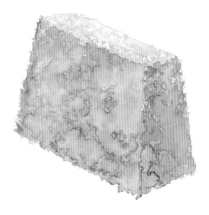

## Best tools to use

Broad-leaved evergreens, such as laurel (*Prunus laurocerasus*), should be cut with secateurs for accuracy, to ensure only whole leaves are removed. Any leaves that are cut in half develop a brown line where the cells have been damaged and these 'half leaves' slowly turn yellow and die. All other types of hedge can be clipped with a pair of shears.

## Hedge clipping

**1** When working with new hedges or hedges that need re-shaping, place an upright post at each end of the hedge and stretch a garden line between them, set it to the desired height of the hedge and start clipping. This will give you a guide to the height without you having to step back all the time, but do beware of cutting through the line!

**2** Always start at the bottom of the hedge and work upwards so that as you cut, the clippings will fall out of the way, making it easier to see where to cut next. If a mechanical hedge trimmer is used, always cut upwards with a sweeping arc-like action, and keep the cutting bar parallel to the hedge. For safety when trimming hedges over 1.8 m (6 ft) in height, use two step ladders with a standing board in between.

**3** Once the hedge has reached the height you require, cut the top down by about 30 cm (1 ft). This will encourage the upper shoots to grow thick and bushy and any woody stumps from the pruning cuts will be hidden by the new growth. Whenever you clip, especially with evergreen hedges, remember to maintain the sloping angle, so that the bottom is slightly wider than the top.

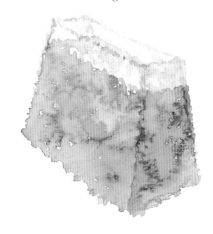

# training fruit trees

There are various methods of growing fruit trees, but generally they are either free-standing or trained. Trained trees are those that are grown into a formal shape and in a single plane, usually against a wall, fence or some other means of support. The purpose of wall-training is to produce high quality fruits in a relatively confined space, and to provide shelter as well as additional warmth for plants, such as peaches and nectarines, that are not fully hardy. Two of the most commonly encountered forms of trained fruit trees are the espalier and the fan.

## *materials & equipment*

*spade*

*secateurs*

*garden twine*

*wire*

*canes*

*fruit tree (see opposite)*

## The fan

With a fan-trained tree the aim is to produce and train a series of lateral or side shoots and their side shoots (sub-laterals), which radiate out in an arc from a short leg or stem. This method is most commonly used for the cherry family, including acid and sweet cherries, apricots, peaches and plums, as well as for figs.

**1** Make a support framework of horizontal wires fixed to the wall at 20 cm (8 in) intervals, the lowest one 40cm (16 in) above soil level.

**2** After planting the maiden tree, just before growth starts in spring, cut back the main stem to a pair of lateral branches about 30 cm (1 ft) above the ground. Remove all other shoots, cutting them close to the main stem.

**3** In the first summer, tie the two lateral shoots to canes set at 45°, raising them if necessary to increase vigour.

**4** In the first winter, cut back the two side branches to a bud about 45 cm (18 in) from the main stem.

**5** The next summer, tie in four shoots on each lateral to angled canes. Cut out other shoots.

**6** In the second winter, cut back each branch to leave 75 cm (30 in) of mature wood.

**7** In the third summer tie in the new shoots that have developed from the second year's growth to form an even shaped fan. Prune back any sub-laterals to avoid overcrowding.

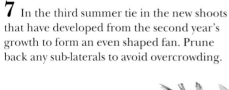

## The espalier

This tree form involves training two or three tiers of shoots at right angles to the main stem.

Horizontal wires, 60 cm (2 ft) apart, form the support framework. Fruits most commonly grown as espaliers are apples and pears.

**1** Plant a maiden whip in late autumn or early winter. As soon as buds appear, cut the main stem back to a bud 45 cm (18 in) from the base.

**2** In the first summer, train the resulting shoots along canes fixed to the wires, angling the two lower shoots at 45° to the main stem; lower these shoots to 90° later in the summer.

**3** In subsequent winters, the central stem is cut back to a cluster of three buds 30 cm (1 ft) above the top tier. Prune back lateral shoots by one third.

**4** In subsequent years, starting in mid-summer, repeat the process, treating the three new shoots arising from the main stem in the same way as those in the first year. Continue until four or five tiers are produced.

**5** Any new lateral growths or spurs on the horizontal or vertical stems should then be pruned regularly in the summer and the leading shoots removed, to promote fruiting.

# topiary

Topiary is the clipping and training of plants into formal shapes. It involves early training followed by repeated restrictive pruning, the frequency of which depends on the intricacy of the design. The real secret to topiary is to prune little and often, constantly checking the plants and trimming them as necessary to form a dense, compact growth habit. Plants grown in pots are particularly convenient subjects for topiary, as they can be brought into the house and used for indoor display, although they will deteriorate rapidly if kept in for more than a few days.

### *materials & equipment*

*pruning shears and secateurs*

*for a cone: 3 bamboo canes, several metres of wire and garden twine*

*for a spiral: thick wire*

*for a ball: bamboo cane and garden twine*

*suitable plants (see opposite)*

## Making a topiary spiral

**1** A spiral can be achieved in two stages, but it will take several years to complete. First trim the plant as for a cone. Once it has reached the required height, wind a thick wire evenly around the cone to act as a guide.

**2** Clipping from the bottom, remove some of the growth around the wire until a spiral channel is formed.

**3** Once a definite spiral is visible, you can remove the wire. Clip new growth regularly to retain the shape.

## Making a topiary ball

**1** This shape can be achieved without the use of a template. In the first season tie the main stem to a cane for support, then trim away the lower shoots.

**2** Cut back the growing tip by one third once the plant reaches the required height. Trim the horizontal branches where necessary to encourage a dense, bushy habit.

**3** Finally, clip the plant into a ball shape, working from the bottom upwards. Tie a length of string to the stem so that you can check that the ball has an even radius all the way round.

### Care and maintenance

● *Do not clip topiary after late summer as soft young shoots are particularly vulnerable to frost damage in the late autumn and winter.*

● *If any stems or branches become damaged or broken, they can be removed with secateurs.*

*In order to conceal any holes quickly, branches can be drawn together and tied with thin plastic-coated wire. The manipulated shoots will soon produce new shoots to fill the gaps, and these can be trimmed as necessary as they develop.*

## Choosing a shape

Most topiary designs are easy to form if a template or framework is used. This will help to avoid accidents such as uneven trimming or, even worse, the removal of the wrong branch. For simple shapes, such as a cone or pyramid, canes can be used for the template; with more complex shapes you may need a framework of wrought iron or chicken wire or a cane and wire structure. Other shapes, such as balls, either single or multiple, can be clipped freehand. Bear in mind that the more elaborate the design, the greater the maintenance required.

## Selecting suitable plants

The plants that make good subjects for topiary must have certain characteristics for the growing and training to be successful. Those that respond well include plants with pliable growth which trains easily, a dense and compact growth habit, and attractive foliage.

---

### Plants suitable for topiary

Aster bush *(Olearia nummulariifolia)*
Barberry *(Berberis darwinii)*
Bay *(Laurus nobilis)*
Box *(Buxus sempervirens)*
Cotton lavender *(Santolina chamaecyparissus)*
English yew *(Taxus baccata)*

False holly *(Osmanthus heterophyllus)*
Holly *(Ilex aquifolium)*
Italian cypress *(Cupressus sempervirens)*
Jasmine box *(Phillyrea latifolia)*
Poor man's box *(Lonicera nitida)*
Privet *(Ligustrum ovalifolium)*
Sagebrush *(Artemisia abrotanum)*

---

## Making a topiary cone

**1** In the first summer, cut back any long vigorous shoots that are spoiling the overall shape. The aim is to encourage the plant to grow as evenly as possible. Apply fertilizer if necessary to ensure the plant is growing strongly before clipping begins.

**2** The following summer, make a framework of bamboo canes and wire. Place the canes over the plant, tie them together at the top and wrap a few lengths of wire around them, spacing these evenly up to the top of the plant.

**3** Shake all of the branches to encourage the longer ones to emerge through the cane and wire framework. Then, using sharp secateurs, clip over the plant, removing any growth that extends beyond the frame.

**4** When the clipping is finished, remove the framework. Next, cut back or pinch out the growing point by one third to encourage the plant to produce side shoots and so become more bushy. This clipping and pinching will need to be repeated at least two or three times each year, depending on the plants used and their rate of growth.

# lawn care

*Summer is the time of year when you can really take advantage of your lawn, and enjoy it to the full, for viewing or sitting on or simply appreciating as a garden feature in its own right. However, there are still plenty of maintenance tasks that require attention.*

*Keeping the lawn looking lush, green and tidy requires more than a little help from the garden enthusiast. For a good quality lawn, regular mowing is essential, and weeds, often carried on the breeze, may establish themselves in the lawn and must be eradicated. A flagging lawn may be in need of an invigorating tonic, in the form of an occasional feed. Any stress suffered due to lack of water must be remedied as quickly as possible and pests and diseases must be kept in check.*

# Mowing
In order to maintain a healthy lawn mowing must be carried out regularly throughout the summer. The best approach is to mow little and often, although the frequency of mowing will depend on a number of factors, such as the amount of summer rainfall, the different grasses used to make up the lawn and how vigorous they are, and the type of lawn required – whether an ornamental backdrop or a hard-wearing play area.

## Mower types

**Cylinder mower**
A scissor-like cutting action traps the grass between moving blades and a lower fixed blade. The number of blades and the speed of rotation determine the fineness of the cut.

**Rotary mower**
The grass is cut by a high speed, horizontally rotating blade, and the cutting height is adjusted by raising or lowering wheels or rollers. This type is useful for cutting longer grass.

**Hover mower**
This type has a scythe-like cutting action identical to that of a rotary mower, but the hover mower is actually held over the grass on a cushion of air, which makes it lighter to use.

## Timing

The mowing season usually lasts from mid-spring through to mid-autumn, peaking in the early summer, when the grass is growing at its fastest annual rate. After this period growth will slow down, as the grass species and cultivars try to produce flower heads and seed. The drier weather conditions also discourage rapid extension growth.

## Weather

The type of mowing practised depends on the prevailing weather conditions. When the weather has been dry for a long period or if it is hot and sunny, mow at a slightly higher setting to leave the grass blades longer and shade their roots. This reduces the stress caused by drought and lessens the amount of watering required. After heavy rainfall mow frequently, but at a high setting. Cutting the grass very short, or 'scalping', weakens the shoots and encourages the establishment of moss and weeds. If the lawn is very wet, a hover-type mower can be run over the grass, either at a very high setting or with the blades removed. This will blow the water from the grass and make it sufficiently dry to mow properly within half an hour.

# Height

Resist the temptation to cut the grass very short in the hope that it will be a long time before it needs cutting again, as this allows moss and weeds to establish themselves while the grass struggles to recuperate. The golden rule is never to reduce the height of the grass by more than one third at a single cut, and always allow the grass to recover for a couple of days before cutting it again.

| Mowing heights and frequencies | | |
|---|---|---|
| Lawn type | Height | Mowings per week |
| Very fine ornamental | 5 mm (¼ in) | 2–3 |
| Average garden | 1 cm (½ in) | 1–2 |
| Hard wearing (play area) | 2 cm (¾ in) | 1 |

# Collecting the clippings

Always remove the clippings from the lawn after mowing, as any left behind seldom decompose fully and form a layer of dead grass, or 'thatch', over the soil. This layer can cause yellow patches, prevents water and fertilizer reaching the roots, harbours pests and diseases, and encourages cast-forming worms. If your mower does not have a box to collect the clippings, remove them with a spring-tine rake. Add them to the compost heap unless the grass has just been treated with chemicals. Bear in mind that taking the clippings away means that more fertilizer has to be used to keep the lawn healthy.

# Edge trimming

The edges of the lawn need to be trimmed regularly to prevent them becoming ragged and untidy. At the start of the season always cut a clean edge to the lawn with a half-moon edging tool; the best time to do this is after the very first mowing of the season.

**1** When cutting a new edge to the lawn, it is easier to achieve a straight line if you use a wooden plank as a guide. Lay the plank on the lawn, close to the edge, and cut against it, clearing the soil and grass away as you work. This should be done only once a year or the lawn will gradually become smaller.

**2** After every mowing, the edge can be trimmed with long-handled shears to remove any grass hanging over onto the border or path. For the best effect, cut the grass back as close to the edge as you can. Always remove the grass trimmings and collect them along with the clippings from the mower.

# Weeding
Weeds not only make a lawn look unsightly, because of their vigorous growth they can also smother and kill the grass. The more established a weed becomes, the more difficult it is to eradicate. Various methods of weeding can be employed – and the sooner the better.

## Mowing to control weeds

Regular mowing will make it difficult for weed seeds blown onto the lawn to establish themselves. Close mowing is effective for controlling many creeping surface weeds, such as clover, daisy, pearlwort, speedwell, trefoil and yarrow, especially if they are spotted before they start to spread. Just before mowing, rake the weeds into an upright position; most of the growth can then be mown off and taken away.

## Weeding by hand

Tap-rooted weeds, or those that form a flat rosette, such as dandelions, plantain, ribwort and thistles, can be dealt with by hand. Use an old knife with a long blade or a small hand fork to dig or cut out the weed, complete with its tap root. Dig deeply to get the whole root; if even a tiny piece is left in the soil, the weed may well regrow.

## Chemical control

The most troublesome lawn weeds are usually too well established to eradicate by mowing or digging out, and you may need to use a selective 'hormone' type weed-killer.

**1** Measure the area affected to find how much weed-killer you need. Pour the chemical into the sprayer and top up with water as recommended by the manufacturer.

**2** Now spray the area to be treated. If only a few weeds are present, you can just spray each one; if the weeds are numerous, work over the whole lawn systematically.

**3** Wash out the sprayer thoroughly after use. Within two or three days the weeds will curl up and they can be killed off by mowing. Do not use these contaminated mowings for compost or mulch, as the chemical residue may be harmful to plants.

# Watering

In an average year a well-kept lawn should be able to survive without watering for at least two thirds of the year. However, in the height of the summer or in long dry periods, the lawn may become stressed due to a lack of water, and irrigation may be needed. The challenge is to spot the first signs of stress and sort out the problem before it becomes acute.

## When to water

A lawn needs to be watered as soon as the first signs of drought start to appear. The symptoms to look for are dull, bluish grass with a hard and fibrous texture and footprints remaining for longer than usual because the grass is limp. If the dry weather persists, the leaves of the grass will gradually shrivel and turn brown and the exposed roots are then in danger of dying off.

## How much to apply

The most common fault is to apply too little water to the lawn, as this encourages the grass to form roots close to the soil surface. These will be the first to dry out in hot weather, making the lawn even more susceptible to drought. Lawns grown on clay soils take much longer to show signs of drought than those grown on light, sandy soils, as clay holds far more water than sandy soil. In the height of summer, in hot, dry weather, a lawn can lose about 2.5 cm (1 in) of water over a week. To replace that would take about 27 litres (4 ½ gallons) of water for every square metre (square yard) of lawn.

## Methods of watering

When watering a lawn, the aim is to replace the water that has been lost in the root zone, rather than on the surface. Wet the soil to a depth of at least 15 cm (6 in); water again when it dries out to a depth of 10 cm (4 in). On very dry soils it is difficult for the water to penetrate and it may form puddles and evaporate, or simply run off on a sloping site. Check the penetration of the water by digging a test hole before and after watering.

To improve drainage on compacted ground, jab the tines of a garden fork into the soil. Work to a depth of 5 cm (2 in) to ensure the hard crust has been thoroughly penetrated.

The most effective method of watering is to use a low-level sprinkler or seep hose, which apply the water slowly and steadily.

# Feeding
Frequent mowing removes organic matter from the lawn and, when the cuttings are taken away, deprives the grass roots of nutrients; this loss has to be replaced, otherwise the lawn will deteriorate. During the summer, it is quite common to see lawns turning pale green or yellow, a sign of nutrient deficiency. This situation can easily be rectified with a fast-acting nitrogen feed, which will provide the lawn with the boost it needs.

## Types of fertilizer

To keep the lawn looking green and lush, apply a fast-acting fertilizer, such as sulphate of ammonia, which is high in nitrogen, causing the grass to change colour in 7 to 10 days. This comes in liquid, crystal or dry form. Be careful not to apply too much as you may scorch the grass, which will then turn brown and die.

## Applying fertilizer

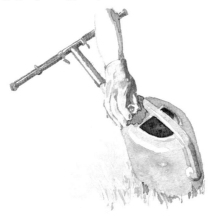

**1** Measure the area of lawn to be fertilized so that you can calculate how much fertilizer is required. Always follow guidelines given by the manufacturer on rates of application.

**2** For a liquid fertilizer, measure the correct amount of chemical concentrate or crystals, and pour it into a watering can fitted with a dribble bar. Top up with warm water, as recommended on the carton.

If the fertilizer is to be applied dry, mix it with soil or sand to avoid scorching the grass. Distribute by hand or fill a special applicator.

**3** Work over the lawn systematically to cover the whole area with fertilizer, and walk at a steady pace to ensure even distribution.

**4** If there is no significant rainfall within two days after applying the fertilizer, water the lawn thoroughly, for at least two hours, to prevent the fertilizer scorching the grass.

# Pest and Disease Control

Grasses, just like other plants, are attacked by various pests and diseases. To make matters worse a lawn consists of vast numbers of grass plants, so once a problem occurs it can quickly reach epidemic proportions. In the late summer, warm, moist conditions may favour fungal and insect activity, and this is the time to be particularly vigilant and act swiftly to keep any infestation under control.

## Diseases

The main lawn diseases are caused by various fungi which, once they take hold, weaken or kill the grasses. Diseases such as dollar spot, red thread and fusarium patch are most likely to occur in late summer, when the soil is warm and the air is moist. They can kill large areas of lawn, leaving bare patches that are open to invasion by weeds and moss.

*Snow mould (Fusarium patch)*

*Red thread (Corticum disease)*

*Dollar spot*

## Pests

There are a few insect pests, such as chafer grubs and leather jackets (the larvae of the crane fly or daddy-longlegs), that may prove troublesome during the summer, mainly because they will feed on the roots of the lawn grasses. The larvae live just below the surface of the soil and nibble away at the roots, causing the grass to turn yellow and wilt in patches. The symptoms produced often look very similar to fungal infection.

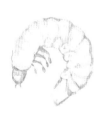

*Chafer grub*

*Leather jacket*

*Damage caused by leather jackets*

## Applying chemical controls

Dollar spot, fusarium patch and red thread can all be successfully treated with products based on carbendazim or dichlorophen. Use insecticides to eradicate chafer grubs and leather jackets. These chemical controls can by sprayed onto the affected area of lawn in the same way as weed-killer (see page 70).

Although chemical controls can be useful, do not rely on them completely. It is important to realize that grass in poor condition is more susceptible to attack, and a regular programme of feeding, watering and checking the weeds should always be the first step to pest and disease control in a lawn.

# planting ground cover

There are a number of perfectly good alternatives to grass for ground cover that look equally attractive and also save on mowing. In shady areas, especially beneath trees, grasses often struggle to survive, but plants such as epimediums, some geraniums, ivies and *Pachysandra* will readily cover the soil. Grass on sloping sites and awkward-shaped areas is notoriously difficult to manage, but plants like baby's tears (*Soleirolia soleirolii*), shown here, *Polygonum affine*, *Rubus tricolor* and thymes all spread and surface-root as they grow, and can be used to cover and stabilize the soil.

## *materials & equipment*

*garden fork*

*weed-killer*

*suitable plants (see opposite)*

*sheets of black plastic to cover the site*

*spade*

*knife*

*trowel*

*organic or inorganic mulch*

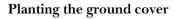

**7** Then take the plant by the root ball and pass it through the plastic into the hole, so the base sits firmly on the bottom of the hole.

**9** Immediately after planting, fold the flaps of plastic back over the soil, so that they sit snugly around the base of the plant.

### Planting the ground cover

**6** Holding each plant by its stem or leaves, gently remove it from the container.

**8** Using a trowel, pull the soil back into the hole and firm gently around the plant. Make sure that the surface of the compost is covered by soil, and leave a slight depression around the stem. Water each plant thoroughly.

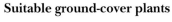

**10** The plastic will need to be covered over to protect it from exposure to the sun, to stop it blowing away and to make the area more attractive while the plants are establishing themselves. Use a layer of organic material, such as bark chippings or wood chips, or an inorganic material, such as gravel. Spread it evenly over the plastic and around the base of the new plants.

---

### Suitable ground-cover plants

**Slow-growing clump formers**
*Alchemilla mollis*
*Brunnera macrophylla*
*Geranium endressii*
*Hebe rakaiensis*
Marjoram (*Origanum vulgare*)
*Nepeta × faassenii*
*Persicaria campanulata*

**Quick-growing colonizers**
*Ajuga reptans*
*Cerastium tomentosum*
*Hedera colchica*
*Hypericum calycinum*
*Luzula maxima*
*Pachysandra terminalis*
*Pleioblastus auricomus*

## Preparing the site

**1** For ground-cover plants to work effectively, the site in which they are going to grow must be well prepared and free from all traces of perennial weeds. Dig over the soil and pull out the weeds, applying chemical weed-killers if necessary.

**2** Lay out the plants, in their containers, over the site, to determine the position of each one. Avoid spacing them too close together or they will soon become overcrowded.

**3** After marking the position of each plant, with a stick or label, remove the pots and dig the planting holes with a small trowel. Each hole should be large enough to accommodate the plant's whole root system.

**4** Before planting begins, place a sheet of heavy-gauge black plastic over the site, cutting it to fit as necessary. Stretch the plastic as tight as you can, then bury the edges, at least 15 cm (6 in) deep, with a spade. It is possible to plant ground-cover plants without using a plastic mulch, but this will involve a great deal of work during the first two years to keep the area free from weeds. Once established, however, the plants cast sufficient shade over the ground to discourage weed seeds from germinating.

**5** The air will be colder where the planting holes have been dug, and this will cause condensation to form on the black plastic sheet directly above them. At each point where you see this, cut a cross in the plastic with a sharp knife. Then you can fold back the flaps to reveal the hole beneath.

# routine care

*It is very tempting to believe that the garden can look after itself through the summer. However, because the weather is an unknown quantity, the main tasks in the garden are an unknown quantity too. A summer that brings wetter than average weather will be one when the plants will need more attention and protec-*  *tion. In dry weather the day-to-day tasks are different and regular watering will be necessary. It is particularly important to keep on top of the routine jobs before going away on holiday, to prevent the garden becoming overgrown and looking neglected. The long summer days offer a wonderful opportunity to take up a project in the garden, such as adapting an old sink for use as an alpine trough and filling it with new plants.*

# Feeding

Very few plants can sustain rapid growth without a 'boost' of nutrients during the growing season, as the development of shoots, stems, leaves and flowers can cause a huge drain on the plant's resources. This depletion is made even worse when flowering plants are dead-headed, and the spent flower heads are taken way, as this deprives the plant of a valuable source of organic matter and nutrients. Unless some replacement nourishment is provided, the plant's performance and vigour will decline.

## Fertilizers

Artificial fertilizers vary greatly in the rate at which they release their nutrients. Described as slow- or quick-release, the essential difference between them lies in how soluble they are in water. The rate of release is also dependent on the size of the fertilizer particles: the smaller they are, the more rapidly they break down.

| Release rates for common fertilizers | |
|---|---|
| **Fertilizer type** | **Plant response** |
| Slow-release (resin coat) | 14–21 days |
| Quick-acting (top-dressing) | 7–10 days |
| Liquid feed (applied to soil or compost) | 5–7 days |
| Foliar feed | 3–4 days |

### Dry feeds
The most common fertilizers come in the form of powder, granules or pellets. They can be used as a base dressing, added to the soil before sowing or planting, or to top-dress established plants, such as shrubs or hungry feeders like chrysanthemums, during the growing season. Before applying a top-dressing, make sure that the soil is moist. The plant will be able to take up the fertilizer most readily if it has already been incorporated into the topsoil.

### Liquid feeds
These come as a liquid concentrate or as granules or powder, which are diluted or dissolved in water. When preparing liquid feeds, it is essential to add the correct amount of water, following the manu-facturer's recommendations. It is also important to mix them thoroughly and to keep the solution well agitated. These soluble fertilizers are applied with a watering can or hose, and are ideal for use on most plants.

### Foliar feeds
These are specially formulated fertilizers used to correct specific nutrient deficiencies or meet particular needs. Sprays containing magnesium will assist fruiting, and iron-based preparations are often used on acid-loving plants, such as azaleas and camellias, which are susceptible to iron deficiency when grown on slightly alkaline soils. Spray foliar feeds onto the leaves only in dull weather, as this reduces the chances of leaf scorch.

# When to feed

Plants growing in containers, such as hanging baskets and window boxes, are particularly vulnerable because their roots are restricted and they have only a limited supply of food. Even if nutrients are present in the soil, they are effective only if the compost is sufficiently moist. The best approach is to apply a regular liquid feed (every 10–14 days) once the plants have started to flower. For plants growing in the garden soil, if they are repeat flowering, feed after the first flush of flowers; if they bloom only once each year, feed after flowering to promote good quality flowers the following year.

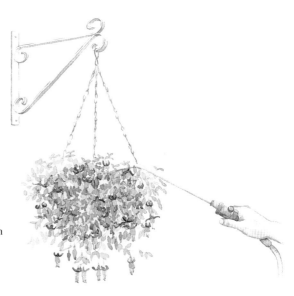

---

### The golden rules of feeding

- Always follow the manufacturer's directions.
- Only feed your plants when they are actively growing.
- Never feed plants that are dry, without

watering the soil or compost first.
- Do not apply fertilizer in bright sunlight, as this can lead to scorching.
- Wash off any concentrated feed that is spilt directly onto the plant.

---

# Composting

Garden compost is another useful source of plant food. Well-rotted plant and animal waste not only provides nutrients (although not the high levels obtained from fertilizers),

it also boosts the activity of earthworms and other beneficial creatures in the soil. Most garden and kitchen waste can be used, but aim for a balance of different materials.

**1** Start by placing a layer of bulky material, such as wood shavings or finely shredded bark, about 10 cm (4 in) deep, in the bottom of the compost bin. A container with a removable front is the easiest to work with.

**2** Next add a layer of green material, such as grass mowings or cabbage leaves, about 20 cm (8 in) deep. Alternating the layers like this will encourage rapid decomposition.

**3** To accelerate the start of the composting process, sprinkle a compost primer over the layers. A cheaper alternative is to add a nitrogenous fertilizer, such as sulphate of ammonia, which will also speed up the composting process. Continue building up the compost heap, adding bulky and green material in alternate layers. After two weeks, turn the heap from top to bottom to allow it to compost evenly.

# Watering
Summer, for most plants, is a time for rapid growth. In order to sustain this the plants need plenty of light and food and copious quantities of water; in particularly hot weather they may need watering twice each day to prevent wilting. Given the huge amount of work this may involve, it makes sense to conserve as much moisture as possible in the soil.

## Signs of water loss

Plants can consist of up to 90 per cent water, which is constantly being lost from pores in the leaves. In dry conditions, the amount of water lost can exceed that taken in by the roots, which causes the plant to wilt. This manifests itself in the shedding of buds, premature drop of flowers or poor colour and size in those that do open, early leaf loss, small fruits and increased susceptibility to attack by pests and diseases.

## Plants most at risk

The more sappy the plant and the softer the growth, the more vulnerable it is to drought. Bedding plants, for instance, will wilt rapidly in dry conditions. Young plants are also especially at risk: these include seedlings and newly planted vegetables, shrubs or trees. Also, plants grown near mature trees, or in the dry soil next to a wall, need to be checked regularly for moisture loss.

## When to water

Choosing the correct time of day to water your plants can make huge savings in the amount of water lost through evaporation from the soil's surface. The soil is cool and the atmosphere is relatively moist in the early morning and late evening, and application then will allow the water maximum time to soak in and be of most use to the plants.

## Preventing dry roots

How much water to apply is difficult to assess, because every soil is different. Always add enough to soak the soil to a reasonable depth, to encourage plant roots to follow the water downwards. Plants subjected only briefly to drought should quickly recover if given a thorough soaking, ideally by allowing water to run gently onto the soil and soak in.

The effects of long-term drought are more difficult to rectify, and the focus should be on measures to prevent it happening. Preparing the soil deeply with organic matter will help, as it provides a reservoir of moisture for roots. Mulching the surface, such as with bark (even black plastic), will reduce moisture loss through evaporation.

# Water distribution

There are a number of specially designed appliances for watering your garden, with some being more suitable for large areas of lawn, and others for watering smaller beds and borders. For single plants, hand application is the easiest method.

**Static sprinklers**
These sprinklers usually consist of a nozzle on the end of a spike that is pushed into the ground. They deliver water in a set pattern over a given area.

**Rotary sprinklers**
Several nozzles on a central pivot rotate in a circular motion. Water coverage is usually very even, and the rotary speed depends on the water pressure.

**Oscillating sprinklers**
A central spray bar with a series of holes in the top and sides is driven by a mechanism run by water pressure, which moves the bar from side to side.

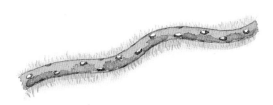

**Rotary-hammer sprinklers**
Ideal for small areas, these are based on a nozzle and counter-balance mechanism, which moves the water jet in a series of short swinging motions.

**Sprinkler and seep hoses**
Perforated hosepipes send out a fine spray over a strip 75 cm (30 in) long. Run at low pressure they allow water to seep out directly into the soil.

**Watering can**
The simplest and most basic method of watering, used for small areas or for young plants and seedlings, which may be damaged by high-pressure jets. A can fitted with a fine 'rose' is the most suitable for delicate plants.

**Water tank**
A useful means of collecting rainwater, essential for watering acid-loving plants in hard water areas.

# Watering plants in containers

A plant in a container is especially at risk from drought as it has no new areas into which the roots can extend to find moisture, so regular watering is essential. Check container plants by feeling the surface of the compost and by lifting the pot – the drier it is and the lighter it feels, the more water it requires. Another useful indicator, for plants in clay pots, is the colour of the pot: if it has become lighter, the compost has dried out.

# Protection
It is not unreasonable to expect the best weather of the year during the summer months, but conditions may still pose a hazard to plants. In addition, pests are often attracted to the colourful and tasty flowers and fruits of this season and deterrents will need to be put in place. Since summer is the main holiday season, measures may also need to be taken to ensure that your plants survive this short period of neglect.

## Protecting blooms

The blooms of some plants are very delicate and are easily damaged by rain, dew and mist, which may mark the petals. For many years, chrysanthemum enthusiasts have 'bagged' their prize blooms, which involves covering the young flower with a greaseproof paper bag as a protection from moisture and dirt. Cover the flower as soon as the bud shows colour – but not before, or the developing flower may become distorted.

## Holiday protection

If you do not want to return to an overgrown, neglected-looking garden after a holiday, make sure you carry out such tasks as lawn mowing, tidying borders, feeding and watering before you leave. Container, house and bedding plants are the most vulnerable, as they have a limited root run and only small reserves of food and water.

### Providing shade
For indoor plants, move the containers away from the windows so that they are not in direct sunlight. Outdoor container plants can be pushed closer together so that they provide shade for one another; grouped like this they will also trap humidity to create their own microclimate.

Larger container plants growing outdoors on a deck or patio can either be moved into a more shaded area, or if they are too heavy to move, a light screen of netting or fleece can be draped over them to filter the sun's rays. Support the netting on canes to avoid damaging the plant.

### Providing water
Small pot plants can be kept moist and humid by placing them on upturned saucers in a bath or sink with 2.5 cm (1 in) of water in the bottom; the pots should not sit in the water or the roots will rot. For larger plants, place a bowl of water beside each one and run a 'wick' of capillary matting or other absorbent material from the water into the compost.

Another method of keeping plants moist is to water the plant well, then place the pot in a polythene bag. Tie the bag around the stem to prevent evaporation and recycle the water inside the bag. You can put the bag over the whole plant, but only use this method for short periods or the plant may start to rot.

# Protecting fruit

For many fruits the need for protection is not just from the elements; more frequently marauding birds will enjoy the best of the season's crop if the ripening fruit is left unprotected. You can grow the fruit inside a permanent cage made with fine mesh wire. Or drape a soft string or nylon mesh over the plants and peg it in place to provide cover until picking has been completed.

| **Fruits that may need covering** | | |
|---|---|---|
| *Blackberry* | *Gooseberry* | *Peach* |
| *Blackcurrant* | *Grape* | *Raspberry* |
| *Blueberry* | *Loganberry* | *Red and Whitecurrant* |
| *Cherry* | *Nectarine* | *Strawberry* |

*Cherry*

*Peach*

*Strawberry*

# Supporting fruit trees

Fruit trees often need another form of protection, as in some years the burden of fruit may be so great that the stem and branches are unable to bear the weight and they may be physically damaged. The easiest way to prevent this is to select a stout stake that is at least 60 cm (2 ft) taller than the tree, and tie it in an upright position to the trunk or main stem. Use a proprietary tree-tie or wrap the stem well with sacking to prevent rubbing or slipping. Run lengths of string from the top of the stake out to the branches, and tie them in place about two thirds of the way along to provide support until the fruit is harvested.

# Protecting low-growing fruit

Low-growing plants often need protection from the soil, to keep them clean and prevent damage from soil-borne pests and diseases. Strawberries produce their fruit very close to the ground; as the berries develop they rest on the soil and are easily attacked by slugs and insects. Straw or plastic laid around the plants, before the berries swell, can overcome most of these problems.

# Pests and Diseases

There is a vast range of pesticides and other chemicals that can be applied to control and eradicate most of the pests and diseases that affect plants, but reaching for the chemical carton should be seen as a last resort. The first course of action should be to practise crop rotation and good general garden hygiene, such as clearing away rubbish and disinfecting tools and equipment, and always to buy healthy plants. Also, regular inspection of plants allows you to spot problems early on, which means that chemicals may be needed only in small quantities.

## Diseases

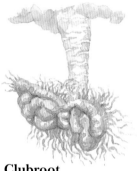

### Botrytis
A fungus that attacks fruits and flowers.
*Symptoms*: a covering of grey felt-like mould; the infected parts of the plant rot and decay rapidly.
*Control:* remove and burn badly affected plant parts, or spray with fungicide.

### Clubroot
A soil-borne fungus, which attacks the roots of plants.
*Symptoms:* swollen distorted roots and yellow wilting leaves, causing the plant to collapse and die.
*Control:* grow resistant cultivars, in well-drained soil; use fungicide on new plants.

### Mildew
A fungus that attacks flowers, fruits, leaves and stems.
*Symptoms:* discoloured, yellow leaves, with white patches on the underside of the leaf, causing slow death.
*Control:* spray with fungicide, grow resistant cultivars and burn any infected plants.

### Rust
A fungal disease that invades the leaves, eventually killing the whole plant.
*Symptoms:* orange-brown spots and yellowing of the leaves and stems; general reduction in growth.
*Control:* grow resistant cultivars, improve air circulation, remove infected plants; apply fungicide.

### Silver leaf
A fungus that enters the woody tissue of members of the plum and cherry family.
*Symptoms:* the leaves take on a silvery sheen, branches die back, and the plant itself gradually dies.
*Control:* prune out infected branches during summer, and remove and burn badly infected trees.

### Virus
This very simple organism lives and feeds on the inside of the plant.
*Symptoms:* yellow distorted leaves and stems, poor weak growth, stunted shoots and striped misshapen flowers and fruits.
*Control:* purchase virus-free plants, control aphids, and burn any infected plants.

# Pests

## Aphids

Large colonies of small sap-sucking insects, which also carry viruses. They range in colour from pale green to greenish black.
*Symptoms:* distorted shoot tips and leaves and a sticky residue on the lower leaves.
*Control:* spray at regular intervals with insecticide but remove and burn badly infected plants.

## Caterpillars

The larvae of butterflies and moths, varying in colour and size.
*Symptoms:* holes eaten in the leaves and young stems, reducing vigour and cropping potential.
*Control:* spray at regular intervals with insecticide or remove by hand.

## Eelworms

Microscopic worm-like pests, which live in the roots, leaves and stems of plants.
*Symptoms:* yellowing of the leaves, stunted growth, wilting and small knobbly swellings on the roots.
*Control:* grow resistant cultivars, in well-drained soil; burn affected plants.

## Maggots

Flies at the larval stage.
*Symptoms:* brown marks and lesions in roots, flowers, fruits, bulbs and stems, often leaving a residue of brown waste on crops.
*Control:* sow crops later, in mid-summer, cover with fleece and apply insecticide at regular intervals.

## Red spider mite

Tiny mites that feed on the sap of plants.
*Symptoms:* yellow stunted growth, curled and mottled leaves covered with a fine webbing; reduced vigour.
*Control:* grow resistant cultivars, maintain good air circulation; use insecticide. Burn badly infected plants.

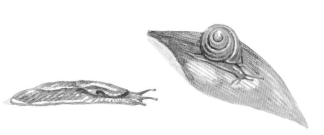

## Slugs and snails

Slugs are tubular, soft-bodied pests, usually black or brown and of varying size; snails are similar but carry a hard shell in the centre of the back.
*Symptoms:* circular holes in the plant tissue, often causing extensive cavities; slime trails may be visible. Seedlings and young shoots are particularly vulnerable.
*Control:* keep the soil well drained and free from weeds and remove all plant debris. Apply a mulch of sharp material such as gravel or soot around the plants as a physical barrier. Pick off by hand at night when feeding. Or use chemical baits or slug pellets. For biological control use a slug nematode.

## Vine weevil

A shiny black weevil, about 2.5 cm (1 in) long, usually only seen on plants in the late evening.
*Symptoms:* semi-circular holes in the leaf margins; the larvae devour plant roots.
*Control:* incorporate insecticide into the soil; for biological control use a nematode to kill the grubs.

# Controlling Weeds

Once plants have become established and started to grow, they will usually sufficiently cover the ground or cast enough shade over the soil to suppress the germination and growth of weed seedlings. Until then, however, nature will need a helping hand, and any weeds that do appear must be removed on a regular basis.

## Weed problems

As weeds grow, they compete with crops and ornamental plants for light, nutrients and water; they can also act as hosts to pests and diseases that may spread to the garden plants. Groundsel, for instance, may harbour the fungal diseases rust and mildew, as well as sap-sucking thrips and greenfly. Chick-weed is a host of damaging red spider mite and whitefly. Some nightshade species host viruses and eelworms that can infect other members of the same family such as peppers, potatoes, and ornamental solanums.

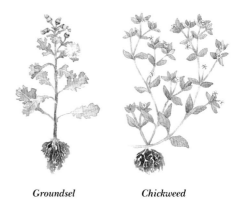

**Groundsel**          **Chickweed**

## Annual weeds

The old saying 'one year's seeds make seven years' weeds' has now been subject of scientific research and, unfortunately, is proving remarkably accurate. Some annual weeds can produce a population of 60,000 viable seeds per square metre (square yard) each year, with the vast majority of these being found in the top 5 cm (2 in) of soil.

---

**Common annual weeds**

Annual meadow grass *(Poa annua)*
Annual nettle *(Urtica urens)*
Black nightshade *(Solanum nigrum)*
Chickweed *(Stellaria media)*
Fat hen *(Chenopodium album)*
Fumitory *(Fumaria officinalis)*
Gallant soldier *(Galansago parviflora)*

Goosegrass *(Galium aparine)*
Groundsel *(Senecio vulgaris)*
Hairy bittercress *(Cardamine hirsuta)*
Ivy-leaved speedwell *(Veronica hederifolia)*
Knotgrass *(Polygonum aviculare)*
Pineapple weed *(Matricaria matricarioides)*
Shepherd's purse *(Capsella bursa-pastoris)*

---

## Perennial weeds

These weeds live for many years, and digging them up is an effective way of dealing with them, as long as every bit of the root system is removed. If only a few weeds are present, dig them out with a trowel or tined implement such as a daisy grubber. Do not throw perennial weeds on the compost heap, as they will simply re-grow; always burn them.

---

**Common perennial weeds**

Bindweed *(Convolvulus arvensis)*
Broad-leaved dock *(Rumex obtusifolius)*
Clover *(Trifolium repens)*
Coltsfoot *(Tussilago farfara)*
Couch grass *(Elymus repens)*
Creeping buttercup *(Ranunculus repens)*
Creeping thistle *(Cirsium arvense)*

Dandelion *(Taraxacum officinale)*
Elderberry *(Sambucus nigra)*
Ground elder *(Aegopodium podagraria)*
Horsetail *(Equisetum arvense)*
Japanese knotweed *(Fallopia japonica)*
Perennial nettle *(Urtica dioica)*
Plantain *(Plantago major)*

---

# Control methods

There are four methods of control available: chemical, where a synthetic chemical is applied over the weeds to kill them; mulching, which involves covering the soil to deprive weeds of light; manual, where weeds are physically removed; and mechanical, which is a method of chopping down or burying weeds using a rotary cultivator.

## Using chemicals

All chemicals used to kill weeds are called herbicides. They are preferred by some gardeners as their main method of weed control, and are certainly the most effective way of controlling persistent perennial weeds. The chemicals are diluted with water and can be applied to plants through a sprayer or watering can with a dribble bar.

## Mulching

Mulching is a very effective method of suppressing weeds. To work well, organic mulches, such as chippings, must be at least 10 cm (4 in) thick so as to block out enough sunlight to prevent weed seeds germinating. Mulches tend to be less effective against established perennial weeds, unless the affected area can be completely covered until the weeds have died out, and new planting is carried out with the mulch in place.

## Manual and mechanical methods

The simplest way to deal with weeds is to remove them physically, by pulling, hoeing or digging them out of the soil. For manual weeding use a hand fork, trowel, daisy grubber or hoe, and for mechanical weeding use a rotary cultivator. The disadvantage of this method of control is that it disturbs the soil, exposing weed seeds to light and so encouraging them to germinate, thus starting the problem all over again. Vigilance is the key: removing weeds as soon as you see them, when they are very young, will cause the least possible disturbance to the soil.

## Combined control

The best way to control weeds is usually a combination of methods, especially where established perennial weeds are a problem. This involves spraying with an appropriate herbicide when the weeds are in full growth; as the weeds start to die, the area is dug over so the weeds are buried in the soil. When the next flush of weeds germinates in response to the ground being disturbed, and the young seedlings emerge, they can be sprayed with a chemical while they are at their most vulnerable and thus be quickly dispatched.

# making a sink garden

Tubs, sinks and troughs of various kinds can be recycled to make excellent containers for plants, and by adding a special coating they can be made to look like natural stone. Alpines provide an excellent display, for many years, in containers such as an old earthenware sink, and are one of the most diverse groups of plants we grow. Low-growing or mat-forming shrubs and conifers are also good subjects, with some covering the surface and others trailing over the rim. Place the sink in position before you start work as it may be too heavy to move once planting is complete.

### *materials & equipment*

*old sink*

*wire brush and mild detergent*

*sponge, sand and water*

*cement, sand and peat*

*stiff-bristled paintbrush*

*pot shards*

*capillary matting*

*free-draining loam-based compost*

*spade*

*hand trowel*

*suitable plants (see opposite)*

*gravel mulch*

**1** Thoroughly clean the sink using a mild detergent and a wire brush, scrubbing the outside and rim of the sink, as well as the inside.

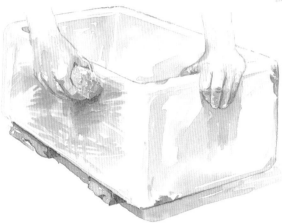

**2** Clean the sink again, including the top and the upper inside edge, using a sponge dipped into a paste made of equal parts fine sand and water. This will scour the surface of the sink and help the coating to bind to it.

**3** To create a weathered stone look, make up a coating using equal parts of cement, sand and peat. Thoroughly mix the ingredients together, then gradually add enough water to form a stiff paste.

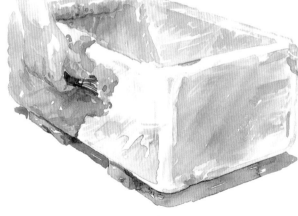

**4** Using an old stiff-bristled paintbrush, spread a 5 mm (¼ in) layer of the coating over the surface of the sink, including the rim and the top 8 cm (3 in) of the inside. Leave the coating to dry.

**5** After two or three days apply a second layer 1 cm (½ in) thick and leave this to dry.

**6** Place a layer of pot shards, 8 cm (3 in) deep, in the bottom of the sink, and cover this with a sheet of capillary matting. This will prevent the compost being washed down into the shards and impeding drainage.

**7** Fill the sink with a free-draining compost. Firm the surface gently with the spade. Top up with more compost as necessary to fill the sink to within 5 cm (2 in) of the rim.

**8** Using a trowel, dig planting holes and place the new plants in them, leaving the top of each root ball slightly high. Firm them in gently.

**9** Position the trailing species near the edges of the sink, so that they can spill over the sides as they grow. During planting, check that each plant has enough room to develop comfortably. Avoid over-crowding, or the plants will have to struggle to survive.

**10** When planting is finished spread a 2.5 cm (1 in) layer of fine gravel over the surface of the compost, in between the plants. To protect the plants while you do this, cover them temporarily with inverted pots. The gravel mulch will help to retain moisture in the compost, improve surface drainage in winter, inhibit the germination of weed seeds and prevent slugs from attacking the plants.

---

### Alpines suitable for growing in sinks and troughs

| | |
|---|---|
| *Arenaria nevadensis* | *Lewisia* hybrids |
| *Carduncellus rhaponticoides* | *Petrophytum caespitosum* |
| *Cyclamen coum* | *Potentilla tommasiniana* |
| *Daphne petraea* 'Grandiflora' | *Ramonda myconi* |
| *Erinus alpinus* | *Raoulia australis* |
| *Gentiana septemfida* | *Salix reticulata* |
| *Helichrysum coralloides* | *Saxifraga* 'Tumbling Waters' |
| *Juniperus communis* 'Compressa' | *Sedum spathulifolium* 'Cape Blanco' |

# pond care

More than any other season of the year, the summer is the time to sit back and enjoy the pond, to savour the movement of water, the antics of the fish and the growth of flowers and plants, both in and around the pond. If only life were that easy! If left to their own devices many of the plants will become too large, crowd-ing out their less vigorous neighbours, so plants have to be lifted and divided, with only the strongest specimens retained. Weeds grow in  abundance, and can easily choke the life out of a healthy pond unless control measures are taken promptly. The water level must be checked regularly, especially in prolonged sunny weather, and fresh water introduced to ensure the pond and its inhabitants remain in peak condition.

# Pond Maintenance

The water of a healthy pond is quite literally alive with masses of microscopic plants. Unfortunately, in the summer some of them can multiply so rapidly that they affect the quality of the water. Weeds are also at their most prolific during this season. Both can have an adverse effect on the pond plants as well as the fish, so keep a watchful eye and resolve any problems as soon as they become apparent.

## Water colour

Brown murky water is often a good sign, as it usually means that the fish are feeding at the the pond bottom or are busily breeding. If the water is blue or black, however, or has a thick whitish scum on the surface and foul-smelling bubbles, it is probably polluted by rotting vegetation at the pond bottom. This robs the water of oxygen, and may kill fish and water snails. The only long-term solution to this is to drain the pond and clean it out.

**1** First remove the fish and plants from the pond and store in buckets of water. Drain the pond using a pump, or siphon off the water.

**2** The debris that has collected in the bottom can then be scooped out and the lining cleaned. Refill the pond, but before returning the plants and the fish, allow the water to settle and warm up slightly.

## Pond water pH

Ideally the pond water should be slightly acid to alkaline, that is between 6.5 and 8.5 on the pH scale. If your water gives a higher or lower reading than this, the plants and fish may suffer. Check the pH level regularly with a special kit. You can use hydrated lime to raise the pH, but add only a small amount at a time to allow the pond life to adapt to the new conditions.

## Water levels

In hot, dry weather, the water level in the pond can drop by as much as 5 cm (2 in) over a week. Topping up the water regularly will help to prevent the liner, especially if it is plastic, cracking in the heat, as well as keeping the fish and plants healthy. When topping up, allow the water to cascade into the pond from a height of about 1 m (3 ft); although this will create a slight turbulence, it will introduce more oxygen into the water.

# Fish care

In addition to monitoring the colour of the water in the pond, watch the movement of the fish to see if there is any change in their behaviour. For example, if the fish come to the surface frequently, it usually means that the water is short of oxygen. If you see the fish rubbing their bodies against the sides of the pond, they may be suffering from a skin irritation, perhaps caused by altering the acidity or alkalinity of the water too quickly.

### Young fish

If there are male and female fish in the pool, tiny young fish ('fry') will often appear in the summer; these look like glass splinters with small bulging black eyes, darting through the water and hiding under foliage. Unfortunately, the parent fish will quite happily devour their own young as fast as they can catch them; so, using a fine net, scoop up as many of the fry as possible and remove them to a holding tank until they are large enough to be returned to the pond,

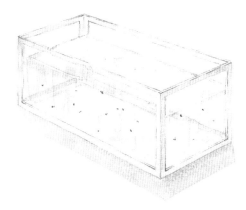

# Weeds

Your pond is likely to provide a perfect environment for weeds as well as for the ornamental plants, and the two will be in fierce competition for light and nutrients.

Both blanket weed and duckweed develop rapidly when light levels are high; if they are not carefully controlled, the condition of the pond can quickly deteriorate.

### Duckweed

This is found growing mainly on still water and covers the surface of the pond, blocking out the light and killing or considerably weakening submerged plants. It is made up of thousands of individual plants, each one consisting of a small cluster of leaves with its root hanging into the water. Remove the duckweed with a fine-mesh net, but do not take it all, as some fish eat it. For a healthy ecological balance, keep at least one third of the water surface free of duckweed.

### Blanket weed

This algae uses light and the nitrogen present in water to grow rapidly. It floats upon the water, smothering the surface of the pond and crowding and choking the ornamental plants. If left unchecked, an infestation of blanket weed can quickly become serious, and at worst may fill the pond from top to bottom. Drag out the weed with a garden rake or a strong stick. If the layers are very thick, you may to need to cut the weed with a knife or a pair of shears as you pull it out (this task will be easier if you have someone to help you). Because the blanket weed will also contain many beneficial insects and water snails, leave the piles of weed beside the edge of the pond overnight to give these creatures a chance to crawl back into the water.

# Summer Plantings

Aquatic plants of all types are best planted in the late spring and early summer, but planting can be delayed until the late summer. Those that are planted later will simply have less time to become established before the winter, although some may not fully recover until the following spring. Choose different types of plants – floaters, oxygenators and deep-water aquatics – to create a balanced environment within the pond, and feed them as they develop to maintain their health.

## Pond and bog plants

For a water feature of any size to be effective and provide the ideal environment for fish and other pond life to live and breed successfully, plants must be present. They provide food, shade and shelter as well as helping to keep the water sweet and clear.

### Deep-water aquatics
Growing up from a depth of about 60 cm (2 ft), these provide shelter for fish and help to keep the water clear.

**Deep water aquatics**
*Aponogeton distachyos*
*Nymphaea*
*Nymphoides peltata*

**Bog plants**
*Lobelia* × *gerardii*
*Matteuccia struthiopteris*

**Floaters**
*Hydrocharis morsus-ranae*
*Lemna trisulca*
*Stratiotes aloides*

**Marginals**
*Calla palustris*
*Juncus effusus* 'Spiralis'

**Oxygenators**
*Chara aspera*
*Elodea canadensis*
*Myriophyllum spicatum*

### Bog plants
These are ideal for a marshy area surrounding the pond as they prefer a rich, peaty, damp soil that will keep their roots cool. Most bog plants are herbaceous perennials and benefit from being lifted and divided every three years or so (see pages 34 to 35).

### Marginals
This diverse group of plants thrives in shallow water or damp soil, depending on the species. Marginals are largely decorative, although they do attract insects, and provide cover for other wildlife.

### Floaters
Plants in this group have their leaves and stems on the pond surface, with their roots submerged. They reduce the amount of light reaching the water and so help to exclude algae.

### Oxygenators
These plants help to keep the water aerated, as they release oxygen as a by-product of photosynthesis. Keep them fully submerged, with only the flowers on or above the water's surface. Aim to include about three oxygenating plants per square metre (square yard) of pond surface.

# Planting water lilies and deep-water aquatics

**1** When planting water lilies or other deep-water aquatics, or replanting divisions of the root (see page 101), trim off any large leaves, otherwise they may cause the plant to lift out of its basket and rise to the pond surface. Also, examine the rhizome and cut away any damaged material, and trim back any fibrous roots.

**2** Line a planting basket with a layer of sacking or thick paper, to prevent the compost from slipping through the mesh. Half-fill the basket with compost.

**3** Make a hole in the centre of the compost and insert the plant, setting it securely on the bottom. Top up with more compost and pack it around the plant. The compost should sit about 2.5 cm (1 in) below the top of the liner.

**4** Cover the compost with a layer of fine gravel, 1 cm (½in) thick. The gravel will stop the compost being flushed out of the basket into the pond. Water the container thoroughly to soak the plant and settle the compost around its roots.

**5** Finally, attach sturdy string handles to the container and lower the plant into the desired position within the pond. Lower the basket slowly to enable it to absorb water at a steady rate, otherwise it may tip over onto its side.

# Feeding plants

If aquatic and marginal plants become starved of nutrients, there is only one definitive answer, which is to lift the plants and replant them in fresh compost. This is not always possible, however, and the alternative is to feed the plants *in situ*. Modern fertilizers used for aquatic plants come in various forms, such as clay balls and pellets; they are also sold in perforated sachets, rather like tea bags.

Whichever type you choose, push the fertilizer into the compost around the plant so that the nutrients reach the roots, rather than being dispersed into the surrounding water. If too much nitrogen is released into the pond, there is always the danger that it could trigger a massive increase in the development of green algae, which will compete with the decorative plants for food and light.

# Propagation
Many water plants will be flowering and growing rapidly in this season, often providing suitable material with which to increase your stocks, whether from seeds or cuttings. Some may even have exceeded their allotted area and will need lifting and dividing into smaller plants to maintain a balanced population and prevent overcrowding. For many of these tasks, the earlier in the summer that they are carried out, the more rapidly the individual plants and the pond as a whole will recover.

## Seed-raised plants

Many of the bog plants and marginals around the edge of the pond can be increased by raising new plants from their seed, collected after flowering. In most cases, these seeds can be sown fresh, immediately after collection, but they may need some protection over the winter; seeds of pickerel weed (*Pontederia*), for instance, will not germinate until the following spring.

### Seed sowing

**1** Select a seed tray (modular trays are best if seedlings are to stay in the tray a long time) and fill with compost. Firm gently to within 1 cm (½ in) of the rim. For very fine seeds sieve a thin layer of compost over the surface.

**2** Sow the seed as evenly as possible over the surface. Place larger seeds individually on the compost and press them in lightly.

**3** Sieve a thin layer of fine compost over the seeds and firm the compost gently. Press very fine seeds gently onto the surface rather than try to cover them with more compost as they may become too deeply buried.

**4** Remember to write the name of the plant and the date the seeds were sown on a label and insert it at the end of the tray.

**5** Place the seed tray in a shallow container of water so that the compost takes up water by capillary action, then allow the surplus water to drain away. This method does not disturb the seeds, making it much safer than overhead watering, with a can.

**6** Cover the seed tray with a piece of clear glass and a sheet of newspaper to provide the seeds with shade and to prevent the compost from drying out. Place the completed tray in a propagating case or a cold frame to provide a warm, humid environment that will encourage the seeds to germinate.

# Cuttings

Many marginal plants can be propagated by cuttings, taken in early to mid-summer. This is particularly useful for the less hardy plants, which can be overwintered as cuttings to ensure that some of the stock survives if the parent plants are killed during cold weather.

**1** Select non-flowering shoots, remove the lower leaves and trim to about 8 cm (3 in) long, cutting just below a leaf joint.

**2** Insert the cuttings into plastic pots filled with loam-based compost, making holes for the cuttings with a dibber or pencil. Stand the base of the pot in a saucer of water to keep the compost permanently wet.

**3** Keep the cuttings in a cool, partially shaded place. For the first week, cover the cuttings with a polythene bag to reduce the risk of the compost drying out.

# Dividing water lilies

## Simple division

**1** Lift the plant to be divided from the pond, then gently remove it from its container. Break the rhizome into two or three sections, each with roots, stems and shoots.

**2** Wash each section of rhizome thoroughly to make sure that all of it is clearly visible. Using a sharp knife, carefully cut away any rotting or diseased sections of rhizome and remove any old or weak-looking stems and shoots. Cut off any dead or damaged leaves.

**3** Cut the healthy divisions into smaller segments. Keep in a bucket of water until ready to replant, to stop them drying out.

**4** Replant the new divisions in containers and then reintroduce them into the pond (see 'Planting water lilies', on page 99).

## Bud cutting

**1** To produce numerous water lily plants from one rhizome, cut off young shoots arising from a growth bud (called 'eyes').

**2** Plant the 'eyes' in small baskets of loam-based compost and submerge in containers of water, so that the compost is only just covered. The following spring, the 'eyes' will be large enough to be planted in the pond.

# pebble pond

A pebble pond with a fountain of water jetting through the centre makes an unusual and attractive feature in any garden, and can be adapted in size to suit the space available. A metal or plastic tank, or even a bin, is simply inserted into the ground to act as a reservoir, and to house the submersible pump; the decorative pebbles are then suspended above it on a metal grille. Add shells to the collection of pebbles if you have any, as the water splashing over them will highlight the shiny surfaces, as well as bringing out any interesting colours or markings.

## *materials & equipment*

*peg and string*

*garden spade*

*hardcore and sand*

*60 x 45 x 10 cm (24 x 18 x 22 in) tank or bin made from plastic or galvanized steel*

*flexible pond liner*

*submersible pump*

*waterproof tape*

*rigid pipe*

*strong metal grille*

*pebbles*

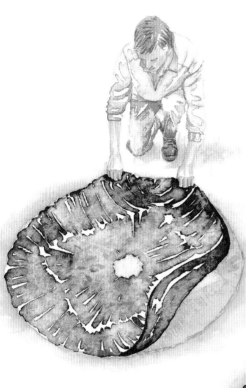

**6** Cut a circle of flexible pond liner 8 cm (3 in) larger in diameter than the circle on the ground, then measure and cut a 15 cm (6 in) diameter hole in its centre, to accommodate the submersible pump. Lay the liner in position, with the hole sitting over the centre of the tank.

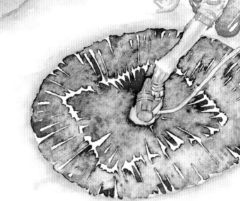

**7** Lower the submersible pump into the tank so that it rests on the bottom. Run the cable from the pump over the liner, fastening it in place with water-proof tape. Connect a length of rigid pipe to the outlet pipe on the pump so that it sits slightly above the level of the tank; this will act as a fountain head.

**8** To provide the support for the pebbles lay a strong metal grille, such as a foot-scraper, or a piece of stout wire mesh, into position across the top of the tank. Where the edges come into contact with the liner, place extra off-cuts of liner underneath the metal to prevent it from puncturing the material. Adjust the grille so that the fountain head on the pump protrudes between the metal bars.

**9** Fill the tank with water, covering over the submersible pump. Switch on the pump to check and adjust the pressure; if your pump will not adjust, raise it on bricks to increase pressure.

**10** Finally, place a layer of pebbles over the grille and the collar of pond liner, filling all gaps. Cut away any excess liner protruding beyond the edge of the circle. Turn the pump on again so that water shoots from the fountain onto the surrounding pebbles, before flowing back into the sunken water tank.

**1** Begin by marking out the shape of the finished pond in your chosen site, which should be clear of all vegetation and large stones. Measure out a circle with a radius of about 60 cm (2 ft) by fixing string of this length to a central peg and marking around it (adjust the radius if you wish to make the pond smaller or larger). You may find it easier to use a trowel to mark the circumference in the soil. Then, using a spade, take off the topsoil to a depth of 8 cm (3 in), within the marked circle.

**2** To make a hole for the tank, mark a rectangle inside the circle; this needs to be about 60 x 45 cm (24 x 18 in), or slightly larger than the tank. Dig this hole to a depth of 63 cm (25 in), or 8 cm (3 in) deeper than your tank. Use a marked stick to check the depth of the hole as you work.

**3** Place a layer of hardcore about 8 to 10 cm (3 to 4 in) deep in the bottom of the hole and ram it in. Cover this over with a layer of sand, to provide a solid base for the tank.

**4** Lower the tank into the pit, so that it sits squarely on the bottom. Make sure that the rim is just below soil level. Fill in the spaces around the outside of the tank with soil, to steady it in position.

**5** Build up the soil on all four sides so that it slopes upwards from the tank to the outer circle. Along the two long sides of the tank flatten the ground to make two strips, 8 cm (3 in) wide; this will form a level base for the grille. Spread a layer of sand over the soil, to act as a buffer for the pond liner.

# Glossary

**Algae**
Primitive plants that usually grow in wet or damp conditions.

**Alpine**
A plant originating from mountainous regions; often applied to rock garden plants.

**Alternate**
Buds or leaves that occur at different levels on opposite sides of the stem.

**Annual**
A plant that completes its reproduction cycle in one year.

**Aquatic**
Any plant that grows in water, whether anchored or free-floating.

**Axil**
The angle between a leaf and stem.

**Axillary bud**
A bud that occurs in a leaf axil.

**Basal**
A shoot or bud arising from the base of a stem or plant.

**Base dressing**
Fertilizer or organic matter incorporated into the soil before planting or sowing.

**Biennial**
A plant that completes its life cycle in two years; it produces roots and leaves in the first year, and flowers and fruits in the next.

**Bleeding**
The excessive flow of sap, usually from plants pruned in spring.

**Bolt**
The premature flowering and seed production of a cropping plant.

**Branch**
A shoot growing directly from the main stem of a woody plant.

**Broad-leaved**
Deciduous or evergreen plants that have flat, broad leaves.

**Bud**
A condensed shoot containing an embryonic shoot or flower.

**Bulb**
A storage organ consisting of thick fleshy leaves arranged on a compressed stem.

**Callus**
The plant tissue that forms as a protective cover over a cut or wounded surface.

**Compost**
A loam- or peat-based potting medium made to a standard formula. Also well-rotted organic matter, such as garden waste.

**Conifer**
Plants that have narrow needle-like foliage and naked ovules often borne in cones.

**Cordon**
A plant (often a tree) trained to produce fruiting spurs from a main stem.

**Crop rotation**
A system of moving crops to improve growth and help control pests and diseases.

**Cultivar**
A plant form originating in cultivation rather than in the wild.

**Cutting**
A portion of a plant used for propagation.

**Dead-heading**
The deliberate removal of dead flower heads.

**Deciduous**
Plants that produce new leaves in the spring and shed them in the autumn.

**Disbudding**
Removal of unwanted buds to produce fewer, but much larger flowers.

**Division**
A method used to increase the number of plants by splitting them up into smaller units.

**Dormancy**
A period of reduced growth, usually from the autumn through the winter.

**Espalier**
A tree trained to produce several horizontal tiers of branches from a vertical main stem.
**Evergreen**
Plants that retain their actively growing leaves through the winter.
**Fan**
A tree or shrub trained to create a network of branches spreading out from the main stem.
**Fertilizer**
An organic or inorganic compound used to help plants grow.
**Fibrous roots**
The fine, multi-branched roots of a plant.
**Formative pruning**
Pruning of young plants to establish a desired plant shape and branch structure.
**Framework**
The main permanent branch structure of a woody plant.
**Fungicide**
A chemical used to control fungal disease.
**Germination**
The development of a seed into a plant.
**Half hardy**
A plant that can tolerate low temperatures but is killed by frost.
**Hardy**
A plant that can tolerate temperatures below freezing without protection.
**Herbaceous**
A non-woody plant with an annual top and a perennial root system or storage organ.
**Inorganic**
A man-made chemical compound (one that does not contain carbon).
**Lateral**
A side shoot arising from an axillary bud.
**Layering**
A propagation technique that encourages roots to form on a stem before it is detached from the parent plant.
**Leader**
The dominant shoot of a plant.
**Maiden**
A young (one-year-old) budded or grafted tree or bush.
**Marginal plant**
A plant that prefers to grow in damp soil conditions or partially submerged in water.
**Mutation**
A plant change or variation occurring by chance, often referred to as a 'sport'.
**Nematode**
Microscopic worm-like organism that can be used to attack specific pests.
**Nutrients**
Minerals in soil or fertilizer that feed plants.
**Opposite**
Where leaves, buds or stems are arranged in pairs directly opposite one another.
**Organic**
Materials derived from decomposed animal or plant remains.

**Oxygenator**
An aquatic plant that releases oxygen into the water.
**Perennial**
A plant with a life-cycle of three years or more.
**pH**
A measure of acidity and alkalinity.
**Pinching out**
The removal (usually with finger and thumb) of the growing point of a shoot to encourage lateral shoots to develop.
**Propagation**
Techniques used to multiply plants.
**Pruning**
Cutting plants to improve their growth or to train them to grow in a certain way.
**Renewal pruning**
A method of pruning based on the systematic replacement of lateral fruiting branches.
**Rhizome**
A specialized underground stem that lies horizontally in the soil.
**Root ball**
The combined root system and surrounding soil or compost of a plant.
**Runner**
A stem that grows horizontally close to the ground, such as in a strawberry plant.
**Sap**
The juice or blood of a plant.
**Scale**
A modified leaf of a bulb used in propagation.
**Shoot**
A stem or branch.
**Shrub**
A woody stemmed plant.
**Side shoot**
A shoot arising from a stem or branch.
**Spur**
A short flower- or fruit-bearing branch.
**Standard**
A tree with a clear stem of at least 1.8 m (6 ft).
**Sucker**
A shoot arising from below ground level.
**Tap root**
The large main root of a plant.
**Tender**
A plant that is killed or damaged by low temperatures, usually 10°C (50°F).
**Tendril**
A thin twining stem-like structure used by some climbing plants to support themselves.
**Top-dressing**
An application of fertilizer or bulky organic matter added to the soil surface.
**Transplanting**
Moving plants from one site to another in order to give them more growing room.
**Whip**
A young (one-year-old) tree with no lateral branches.
**Wilt**
The partial collapse of a plant due to water loss or root damage.

# Useful Addresses

## Nurseries and Garden Centres

**Blooms of Bressingham**
Bressingham
Diss
Norfolk IP22 2AB

**Bridgemere Nurseries**
Bridgemere
Nantwich
Cheshire CW5 7QB

**Burncoose Nurseries**
Gwennap
Redruth
Cornwall TR16 6BJ

**The Chelsea Gardener**
125 Sydney Street
London SW3 6NR

**Clifton Nursery**
5a Clifton Villas
London W9 2PH

**Kennedy's Garden Centres**
Kennedy House
11 Crown Row
Bracknell
Berks RG12 0TH

**Kinder Garden Plants**
Sunnyfield Nurseries
Wragg Marsh
Spalding
Lincs PE12 6HH

**Scotts Nurseries**
Merriott
Somerset TA16 5PL

**The Van Hage Garden Company**
Great Amwell
Herts SG12 9RP

**Wyevale Garden Centres**
Kings Acre Road
Hereford HR4 0SE

## For Hedges, Trees and Shrubs:
**Beechcroft Nurseries**
Appleby
Cumbria CA16 6UE

**Crowders Nurseries**
London Road
Horncastle
Lincs LN9 5LZ

**Hillier Nurseries**
Ampfield House
Ampfield
Romsey
Hants SO51 9PA

**Ian Roger**
**RV Roger Ltd**
The Nurseries
Pickering
N. Yorks YO18 7HG

**Rolawn (Turf Growers) Ltd**
Elvington
York
N. Yorks YO4 5AR

**Weasdale Nurseries**
Newbiggin-on-Lune
Kirkby Stephen
Cumbria CA7 4LX

## For Clematis:
**Bushey Fields Nursery**
Herne
Herne Bay
Kent CT6 7LJ

## For Roses:
**David Austin Roses Ltd**
Bowling Green Lane
Albrighton
Wolverhampton
West Midlands WV7 3HB

**Mattock's Roses**
The Rose Nurseries
Nuneham Courtenay
Oxford
Oxfordshire OX44 9PY

## For Aquatics:
**Anglo Aquarium Plant Co**
Strayfield Road
Enfield
Middlesex EH2 9JE

**Stapeley Water Gardens**
London Road
Stapeley
Nantwich
Cheshire CW5 7LH

## For Bulbs:
**Jacques Amand Ltd**
Clamp Hill
Stanmore
Middlesex HA7 3JS

**Van Tubergen UK Ltd**
Bressingham
Diss
Norfolk IP22 2AB

**Winchester Bulbs**
Winnal Down Farm
Alresford Road
Winchester
Hants SO21 1HF

## For Seeds:
**Basically Seeds**
Risby Business Park
Risby
Bury St Edmunds
Suffolk IP28 6RD

**Johnsons Seeds**
London Road
Boston
Lincs PE21 8AD

**Mr Fothergill's Seeds**
Gazeley Road
Kentford
Newmarket
Suffolk CB8 7QB

**Marshalls**
SE Marshall & Co Ltd
Regal Road
Wisbech
Cambs PE13 2RF

**Suttons Seeds Ltd**
Hele Road
Torquay
Devon TQ2 7QL

**Unwins Seeds Ltd**
Mail Order Dept
Histon
Cambridge
Cambs CB4 4ZZ

## For Trellis:
**Stuart Garden Architecture**
Burrow Hill Farm
Wiveliscombe
Somerset TA4 2RN

# Fertilizers and Mulches

**Miracle Garden Care Ltd**
Salisbury House
Wayside Park
Catteshall Lane
Godalming
Surrey GU7 1XE

**Phostrogen Ltd**
28 Parkway
Deeside Industrial Park
Deeside
Clywd CH5 2NS

**William Sinclair Holdings**
Firth Road
Lincoln
Lincs LN6 7AH

## For Fleece:
**Agralan Ltd**
The Old Brickyard
Ashton Keynes
Swindon
Wilts SN6 6QR

**Agriframes Ltd**
Charlwoods Road
East Grinstead
Sussex RH19 2HG

# Building Supplies

**B&Q plc**
1 Hampshire Corporate
Park
Chandlers Ford
Eastleigh
Hants SO53 3YX

**Garden & Security
Lighting**
1 Yew Tree Walk
Clifton
Beds SG17 5HN

**Harcros Timber & Building
Supplies Ltd**
Harcros House
1 Central Road
Worcester Park
Surrey KT4 8DN

**Homebase**
Beddington House
Wallington
Surrey FN6 0HB

**Leisuredeck Ltd**
Maylands House
Maylands Avenue
Hemel Hempstead
Herts HP2 7DE

# Tools and Equipment

**Black & Decker**
Bath Road
Slough
Berks SL1 3YD

**Butyl Products**
Unit 11
Radford Crescent
Billericay
Essex CM12 0DW

**Capel Manor Horticulture
& Environmental Centre**
Bullsmoor Lane
Enfield
Middlesex EN1 4RQ

**Gardena (UK) LTD**
Dunhams Lane
Letchworth
Herts SG6 1BD

**H S S**
Willow Lane
Mitcham
Surrey CR4 4TS

# Credits

l. = left, **c.** = centre, **r.** = right, **t.** = top, **b.** = bottom

The photographer, Anne Hyde, wishes to make the following acknowledgements: Peter Aldington, Garden Designer of Turn End, Haddenham, Bucks; Margaret Easter, Harpenden, Herts; Lucy Sommers, 13 Queen Elizabeth Walk, London; Ivan Meers and David Boyer; Heather Montgomery, Wisteria Cottage, Maidwell, Northants; Mr and Mrs Siggers, Wichert, Ford, Bucks; Mr and Mrs Try, Favershams Meadow, Bucks; Vanessa and Vinda Saax; Mrs Huntingdon, The Old Rectory, Sudborough, Northants; Mr and Mrs Coote, 40 Osler Road, Oxford; Charles Paddick; Mr and Mrs Fuller, The Crossing House, Shepreth, Cambs; Capel Manor, Enfield, Herts; Clifton Nurseries, Clifton Villas, Little Venice, London.

All photographs taken by Anne Hyde except for the following: p. 10 **c.**, p. 11 **l.**, p. 23 **t.**, p. 24, p. 27, p. 34 **l.**, **c.**, **r.**, p. 35 **r.**, p. 45 **l.**, **r.**, p. 48 **l.**, **r.**, p. 50 **l.**, **r.**, p. 85 **l.** Jerry Harpur. p. 10 **l.** Jerry Harpur – Beth Chatto. p.35 **l.**, p.53 **r.** Marcus Harpur. p.50 **c.** Steve Robson.

# Index

*Page numbers in italics refer to illustrations.*

*Acanthus*, planting 15
*Acer palmatum* (maple) *53*
algae 97, 98, 99
alpine garden, making 90–92
*Amaryllis belladonna 10*
annuals
  cutting back 45
  dead-heading 26, 45
  disbudding 45
  pinching out 44
  sowing 12–13, 25
  summer bedding scheme 24–26
  supporting 44
  thinning 44
  transplanting 12, 13, 26
aphids 18, 87
apples, espalier-grown 59
apricots, fan-trained 60
aquatic plants
  deep-water 98
  floaters 98
  oxygenators 98
  planting 99
*Aquilegia* (columbine) 45
*Aquilegia vulgaris 13*
*Azalea*, feeding 80

baby's tears *see Soleirolia soleirolii*
barberry *see Berberis*
bay tree 20
beans,
  broad 18, 19
  runner 18, 19
bedding, summer
  planting scheme 24–26
*Berberis* (barberry) *21*

*Betula pendula* (birch) *53*
biennials
  sowing 13
  transplanting 13
birch *see Betula*
birds, protection against 25, 85
blackberries 55
blanket weed 97
bog plants 98
*Botrytis* 86
box *see Buxus*
bulbs
  collecting 32, 33
  dividing 35
  lifting 10
  planting 10–11
  scaling 36–37
  supporting 11
*Buxus* (box) *21*

*Camellia* 20, 80
carnations, layering 38
*Catalpa bignonioides* 'Aurea' *23*
caterpillars 87
cauliflowers, harvesting 19
*Chaenomeles*, pruning 46
cherries *85*
  fan-trained 60
  protecting 85
  disease 54
*Chrysanthemum*
  feeding 80
  pinching out 44
  protecting flowers 84
citrus fruits, in containers, 20
*Clematis* 'Lasurstern' *45*
*Clematis 48*
  layering 39
  pruning 48
climbers, pruning 48–49

clubroot 86
*Colchicum* 'The Giant' *10*
columbine *see Aquilegia*
compost heap, making 81
container gardening 20–21
container plants 20–21
  alpines 90–92
  watering 83, 84
containers
  adapting 21, 90–92
  choosing 21
*Cornus alba 23*
*Cotoneaster*, pruning 48
cuttings
  heel 30
  nodal 30
  semi-ripe 30–31
  softwood 30, 101
*Cyclamen hederifolium 10*
cypress 53

daffodil *see Narcissus*
*Dahlia*, pinching out 44
damsons 54
dead-heading 45, 51
*Deutzia*, pruning 46
*Digitalis* (foxglove) 45
disbudding 45, 51
diseases 54, 86
  lawn 73
division 34–35
  fibrous-rooted plants 34
  rhizomatous plants 35, 101
duckweed 97

eelworms 87
*Epimedium* 74
*Epimedium × rubrum 34*
*Erigeron* 45
*Escallonia 48*

espaliers, training 58, 59
evergreens, broad-leaved 52

fans, training 58, 60
fertilizers 72, 80–81
  applying 72, 81
figs, fan-trained 60
fir tree 53
firethorn *see Pyracantha*
flag iris *see Iris germanica*
floating plants 98
flowers, protecting 84
*Forsythia*, pruning 46
foxglove *see Digitalis*
*Fritillaria* 36
fruit trees
  dwarf pyramid 54
  pruning 54–55
  supporting 85
  training 54, 58–60
fruit, protecting 85

*Geranium* 'Johnson's Blue' *14*
geraniums, as ground cover 74
*Gladiolus*, supporting 11
*Gladiolus tristis* 'Bowlby' *10*
golden rain *see Laburnum*
greenfly 88
greengages 54
ground-cover, planting 74–76

hedge trimmers, using 57
hedges 56–57
herbs, harvesting 19
holly *see Ilex*
hosepipes 83
*Hosta*, planting 15

house plants
  holiday care 84
  shading 84
  watering 84
*Hydrangea* 'Blue Wave'
  *31*

*Ilex* (holly) *47*
*Iris germanica* (flag iris)
  dividing 34, 35
ivy, as ground cover 74

knives, pruning 43

*Laburnum* (golden
  rain) *53*
*Lathyrus odoratus* (sweet
  pea) *45*
  supporting 44
laurel *see Prunus
  laurocerasus*
lawn mowers 68
lawns 65–73
  drainage 71
  edge trimming 69
  feeding 72
  mowing 68–69
  pests and diseases 73
  sprinklers for 71, 83
  watering 71
  weeding 70
layering 38–39
  natural 39
  serpentine 39
*Lilium* (lily)
  propagating 33, 36
  supporting 11
*Lilium candidum 10*
*Lilium* 'Enchantment'
  *10*
*Lilium lancifolium 35*
*Lilium martagon 35*
loganberries 55
loppers 42
Lorette System,
  Modified (pruning)
  54
*Lupinus* (lupin) *13*

maggots 87
*Magnolia × soulangeana
  23*
maple *see Acer*
marginal plants, for
  ponds 98
mildew 44, 86, 88
mulches
  black plastic 17, 75,
    82
  gravel 76, 92, 99
  organic 76, 82, 89
mullein *see Verbascum*

*Narcissus* (daffodil)
  propagating 35, 37
nectarines, fan-trained
  60

onions, harvesting 19
oxygenators, pond 98

*Pachysandra* 74
*Paeonia lactiflora 45*
*Passiflora caerulea 31*
peaches *85*
  fan-trained 60
pears, espalier-grown
  59
peas 18, 19
perennial border,
  planning 14–15
perennials, planting 15
*Persicaria bistorta*
  'Superba' *34*
pests 87
  lawn 73
*Philadelphus*, pruning
  46
pickerel weed *see
  Pontederia*
pinching out 18, 44,
  47
pine 53
*Pinus mugo* 'Winter
  Gold' *21*
plums 54, 55
  fan-trained 60
*Polygonum affine* 74
pond (pebble), making
  102–104
pond plants 98
  feeding 99
  propagating
    100–101
pond weeds 97
ponds 93–101
  cleaning out 96
  draining 96
  fish care 97
  topping up 96
  water quality 96
*Pontederia* (pickerel
  weed) 100
pricking out 12
*Primula*, dividing 34
propagation 27–39
  bulb scaling 36–37
  collecting bulbils 33
  collecting seed 32
  creating bulbils 33
  cuttings 30–31, 101
  division 34, 35, 101
  layering 38–39
  pond plants 100–101
  sowing seed 13, 16,
    25, 100
pruners 42
pruning 40–57
  tools 42–43
  climbers 48–49
  fruit trees 54–55,
    58–60
  hedges 56–57
  principles 43
  roses 50–51
  shrubs 46–47, 48
  soft fruits 55
  topiary 61–64
  trees 52–53
  wall shrubs 48–49
  wisteria 49

*Prunus laurocerasus*
  (laurel), pruning 57
*Pulmonaria* 'Blue
  Ensign' *34*
*Pyracantha* (firethorn)
  *47*, 56
raspberries 55
red spider mite 87
*Rhododendron*, in
  containers 20
*Rosa* 'Albertine' *50*
*Rosa* 'Goldfinch' *50*
*Rosa* 'Sanders' White'
  *50*
*Rosa rugosa 47*, 56
roses
  dead-heading 51
  disbudding 51
  pruning 50–51
  rambling 50
  removing suckers 51
*Rubus tricolor* 74
*Rudbeckia fulgida 14*
runners 39
rust 86, 88

salad crops
  harvesting 19
  sowing 16
sap, bleeding 43, 47, 53
saws, pruning 43
secateurs 42
seed
  collecting 32
  sowing outdoors 13,
    25
  sowing under glass
    100
  storage life 32
shears
  edging 69
  hand 43
  hedge trimmer 43,
    57
shrub border, planning
  22–23
shrubs
  in containers 20–21
  for hedges 56
  pruning 46–47, 48
  topiary 61–64
silver leaf 54, 86
sink garden, making
  90–92
slugs 87
snails 87
*Soleirolia soleirolii*
  (baby's tears) 74, *74*
sprinklers 83
stone effect, creating
  90–92
strawberries, protecting
  85, *85*
suckers 51, 55
sweet pea *see Lathyrus
  odoratus*

*Thuja orientalis 31*
thyme 20
  as ground cover 74

tomatoes 18, 19
topiary 61–64
training
  annuals 44
  climbers 44, 48
  fruit trees 54, 58–60
  roses 50
  soft fruits 55
  topiary 61–64
  vegetables 18
  wisteria 49
transplanting 12, 13,
  17, 26
trees
  conifers 53
  deciduous 53
  evergreen 52
  fruit 54, 58–60, 85
  in containers 20–21
  pruning 52–53

variegated plants,
  reversion 52
vegetables
  harvesting 19
  planting 16
  protecting 18
  sowing seed 16
  successional sowing
    16
  transplanting 17
*Verbascum* (mullein) 45
vine weevils 87
viruses 86

water lilies
  dividing 101
  planting 99
watering 82–83
  lawns 71
watering cans 83
weed control 88–89
  chemical 89
  manual 89
  mechanical 89
  mulching 89
  lawns 70
weeds
  annual 88
  lawn 70
  perennial 88
*Weigela*, pruning 46
wilting 82
*Wisteria 48*
  layering 39
  pruning 49
wound paints 43

111

# Acknowledgements

On completing this book, I would like to thank a whole host of
people, who made up the 'team'. I am particularly grateful to Toria
Leitch for setting me impossible deadlines; my wife Val Bradley
for keeping a straight face while checking my grammar, and my
sons Christopher and Nicholas for being so patient.
I would also like to thank Anne Hyde for her excellent photographs
and Ashley Western and Prue Bucknall for their design input.